WHICH WAY TO JESUS?

**Sermons For Lent
and Easter, Cycle B
Gospel Texts**

Harry N. Huxhold

CSS Publishing Company, Inc., Lima, Ohio

Copyright © 1996 by
CSS Publishing Company, Inc.
Lima, Ohio

Scripture quotations are from the *New Revised Standard Version of the Bible*, copyright 1989 by the Division of Christian Education of the National Council of the Churches of Christ in the USA. Used by permission.

Library of Congress Cataloging-in-Publication Data

Huxhold, Harry N.
    Which way to Jesus? : sermons for Lent and Easter : Cycle B, Gospel texts / Harry N. Huxhold.
        p.   cm.
    ISBN 0-7880-0793-9 (pbk.)
    1. Lenten sermons. 2. Eastertide — sermons. 3. Bible. N.T. Gospels — Sermons. 4. Sermons, American. I. Title.
BV4277.H884   1996
252'.62—dc20
                                                                        96-4050
                                                                        CIP

This book is available in the following formats, listed by ISBN:
        0-7880-0793-9   Book
        0-7880-0794-7   IBM 3 1/2
        0-7880-0795-5   Mac
        0-7880-0796-3   Sermon Prep

PRINTED IN U.S.A.

To our Grandchildren
so that one day
they will remember
how Grandfather preached
THE WAY TO JESUS

Table Of Contents

C — Revised Common Lectionary; RC — Roman Catholic Lectionary

Introduction

The church year represents one of the better traditions of the Christian community. Through the years the church year has survived alterations, revisions, and additions. If the present liturgical scheme of worship has one failing, it still betrays its inability to shed some of the rubrics that are better suited for an ecclesiastical community housed in an institution or for a primitive community blessed with considerable leisure.

If the latest revision of the church year boasts a significant change for the better, it is the introduction of the three year lectionary. The revision of the historic pericopes and the addition of two sets of prescribed lessons has enhanced the preaching of the church considerably and enlarged the opportunities for the preacher.

What remains constant in the church year, medieval or contemporary, is the rehearsal of the life, death, and resurrection of our Lord Jesus Christ. The pericopes for Lent and Easter remind us again that the Christ Event through Calvary and the Empty Tomb are the heart of the Gospel and should color the preaching of the Gospel the year through.

God bless the efforts of the preacher as she or he struggles with these texts and improves on the offerings submitted here.

Harry N. Huxhold

Beware Of
Your Piety

Whatever happened to Lent? It has been some time now since church attendance was swollen during this season. Congregations also conducted weekday services that were well attended. Lenten reading was popular, and people talked a great deal about their Lenten fasting. "What did you give up for Lent?" was a common question. Very often that was done with little thought. In the Chicago area in the '50s, where and when Lenten piety was quite prominent, a woman was shopping at the bakery. While she was waiting her turn to be served, a young lad told her he was going to buy some brownies instead of cream puffs. That, he said, was his Lenten sacrifice. The woman suggested that was not much of a sacrifice for Lent. The boy said, "Lady, you don't know how much I like cream puffs."

In a way, the boy's answer illustrates the problem of dealing with the matter of fasting and sacrificing in Lent. The home journals that feature Lenten dishes without meat can produce some very tasty recipes that make the fasting very attractive. Much that has passed as Lenten fasting and sacrifice has been no more than superficial. However, on the other hand, the more obvious complete neglect of Lent on the part of a good number of Christians raises the issue of whether we should not be much more aware of our Lenten piety.

The History

Our observance of the season of Lent has its roots in the early church. Two early church fathers, Augustine and Tertullian, related that the Lenten fast originated with the Apostles. However, the fast of which they wrote was neither the season nor the fasting that we know. What the fathers were undoubtedly referring to was the desire of the early Christian community to sense anew the deep sorrow and pain they experienced during the period that our Lord lay in the tomb. The time was calculated as forty hours and was suggested, therefore, to be the appropriate span for fasting. There also appears to be some evidence that even prior to the suggested forty-hour fast, Christians fasted on Wednesday and Friday. The first fast was a reminder of our Lord's betrayal, and the second the remembrance of his crucifixion.

However, each Sunday was regarded as the Lord's Day, a little Easter, in which both the crucifixion and the resurrection of our Lord were observed. In time, however, as people fixed more and more on the need to consider why our Lord was crucified, the stress was placed on the need for contrition and repentance. Soon the Lenten period was extended to a week, then to two weeks. Ultimately, the forty hours were extended to forty days. At one time this was a period of eight weeks of five days of fasting. By the seventh century the time was calculated as six weeks, not counting the Sundays, which were excluded as days of fasting. That is how we still reckon the period for our observance which began last week with Ash Wednesday.

Lenten Piety Is Personal

How then are we to use these forty days? One can argue that the suggestion of a forty day period of concentration on the passion of our Lord as atonement for our sins does not seem too appropriate in an age in which people generally do not have a deep sense of guilt. Dwelling on the passion of our Lord to heighten the sense of guilt may have worked in the Middle Ages when both the church and the society were so legalistic. However, that does not have much appeal in an age when people are constantly explaining away their guilt or relieving it by some psychological do-it-yourself exercises. Then again the whole pattern of a period of remembrance may have worked well for the calendar of medieval monks and even for horse and buggy days, but it does not fit the era of jet flights and cellular phones. In an age of stress, perhaps the best that one can expect of people for a spiritual observance is that they watch a rerun of *The Ten Commandments* sometime in the forty day period.

To be sure, no one should dictate how one is to conduct pious observances. The Apostle Paul taught that one should not judge us in respect of a holy day. Our Lord taught the same. The text before us is a portion of the Sermon on the Mount. This section has to do with how our Lord's followers were to express their piety. Jesus began on the note that the believers are to express their faith in a personal fashion. Jesus began, "Beware of practicing your piety before others in order to be seen by them; for then you have no reward from your Father in heaven." Jesus was reacting to the kind of public displays of piety that had been prominent in the Hebrew community. Pharisees, in particular, were most demonstrative in their worship and prayerful activity. Jesus found such piety highly offensive in spite of the fact that it appeared so attractive and ordinary people felt the pressure to emulate it. Jesus opposed worship that was designed to impress others and encouraged his followers to make their worship a personal relationship with God.

Lenten Piety Reaches Upward

Lenten piety reaches upward to the Heavenly Father. Each of the prescriptions Jesus gave for wholesome worship were rounded out by a phrase taking note of the Heavenly Father's concern for what we do. Jesus repeats the observance that "your Father sees in secret" and "your Father knows." Jesus does not say this to frighten us into good behavior. Nor does he mention this to make us all the more self-conscious. There are some people who can confess to you that they love their fathers dearly but are all thumbs or trip over their own feet when their fathers walk into the room. Jesus does not want us to think that way about the Heavenly Father.

You are not to be nervous about the fact that God may be looking over your shoulder. When Jesus says that "your Father sees in secret," he means that you are absolutely free to concentrate on what has to be done. God will take note of what you are doing, but as one who is cheering you on to do what has to be done. We do not have to waste one ounce of energy or one breath in trying to impress God or to impress others. To look upward is to look to God for help and the assurance of his support in getting done what has to be done. God will reward those efforts in the proper way and at the proper time.

Lenten Piety Is Sacrificial

Lenten piety is sacrificial. Jesus in no way discouraged sacrificial giving. What Jesus said about giving was, "Whenever you give alms, do not sound a trumpet before you, as the hypocrites do in the synagogues and in the streets, so that they may be praised by others. Truly I tell you, they have received their reward. But when you give alms, do not let your left hand know what your right hand is doing." Fund raisers and development officers rely very heavily upon the publication of the lists of donors. They create all kinds of lists and many categories to be sure that people will see their names in print among the donors, contributors, patrons, sustainers, and friends. Of course, the real reason donors want to see their own names is to be sure that others will see their names. Jesus says that such giving has its own reward. The people who give for the purpose of being noticed by others do get what they want. They are noticed by others.

However, when people give in the unselfish manner of which Jesus speaks, they get the job done. They are able to concentrate on what is needed and who needs what. They do not have to worry about even recognizing themselves in the act. They lose themselves in thinking about those for whom they give. The congregation that exercises its stewardship without having to nail plaques all over its walls, furnishings, and accoutrements to give credit to someone encourages its members to observe what our Lord has to say about sacrificial giving. What is more important is that the dear people who practice this kind of sacrificial giving enjoy the

12

freedom of being able to do for those in need or their favorite causes without having to worry about who notices and whether even they themselves have had a sense of reward. God takes care of all the rewards.

Lenten Piety Is Self-Denial

Not only is Lenten piety sacrificial, but it also calls for self-denial. Jesus certainly was not opposed to the practice of fasting. Fasting is a wholesome practice if pursued properly. What Jesus criticized was the custom of going through such rigorous fasting ordeals that the one who fasts can draw the sympathy and applause of others. Again Jesus says that such fasting will not go unrewarded. People will notice. However, there may be a price to pay. Not only will the one fasting derive some benefit from the purgation that fasting does provide, but the rigorous fasting that produces the disfigurement of the face might also develop other ailments of the body.

Luther was one who suffered in his later years from a host of ailments induced by his intense observance of fasting and other forms of self-denial in his earlier years as a monk. Jesus does encourage fasting. But he encourages his followers to put oil on their heads and wash their faces when they fast. What he meant by that was that his followers should practice good health rules. Fasting is one of them. We all have to struggle with our diets. However, we should also practice all other good forms of hygiene and physical culture. Keeping fit is not a means of trying to please God or atoning for our sins. It is one more form of piety to express our freedom as the children of God in taking good care of our physical condition. The experts would also add that this is the primary and best way for us to achieve healthcare reform.

Lenten Piety Is For Eternity

Lenten piety is for eternity. Jesus said, "Do not store for yourselves treasures on earth, where moth and rust consume and where thieves break in and steal; but store for yourselves treasures in heaven, where neither moth nor rust consumes and where thieves do not break in and steal. For where your treasure is there your heart will be also." Most certainly a basic feature of our piety should be the opportunity to get our priorities straight. To rehearse anew the passion, death and resurrection of our Lord Jesus Christ is to remind ourselves that we are destined for eternity. What we do here upon this planet earth is related to where and how we spend eternity. To measure our lives only in terms of what we possess, what we can amass, and what we want to acquire of material things will frustrate us now and eternally. The hell of it will be that the life we treasured will be no more. Eaten by the ravages of time and robbed of worth and beauty by immeasurable numbers of enemies, the pain of that hellish frustration will be unbearable.

To lay treasures in heaven is to believe and trust that the God who created heaven and earth fashioned a life for eternity that was spoiled and warped by a humanity that thought it could be god-like and content forever by worshipping the things of the creation. However, God was willing to redeem the creatures by restoring to them their innocence by making it possible for them to trust the Creator again rather than the creature. That is what the passion of our Lord affords us. We are led to examine anew what really counts in life. In the Suffering Servant, our Lord, we learn that we can lose everything, life itself, as Jesus did at the cross, and still gain heaven.

Observe Lent

To be sure, what our Lord taught in the Sermon on the Mount about piety was not specifically about Lenten piety. What Jesus said should govern all of our piety. Consequently, how we keep the season of Lent should be shaped by his directives. We recognize that we should avoid the legalism, superficiality, and the showiness of medieval forms of piety. Above all, we do not want to assume the notion that whatever we do will somehow earn the good favor of our Heavenly Father. Instead, we follow the guidelines our Lord gives us for the practice of our piety. When we do that we look upon the season as an opportunity.

In freedom, we begin by noting that our Lenten worship and devotion is meant to deepen our relationship with God. However, as we deepen that relationship, it is because God affords us the opportunity to concentrate completely on what has to be done. God's part in our piety is to strengthen and encourage us. When we think of Lenten sacrifice and denial, the same is true. The sacrifice is focused not on how well we are doing, but what needs to be done. Self-denial in Lent for us is the occasion for us again, not to impress others, but to engage in that kind of introspection and physical training that help us to be fighting trim against all the evil forces and enemies that threaten our relationship with God. The kind of piety which our Lord prescribes for us does suit us up for eternity.

Resist
Temptation

The Holy Gospel for this First Sunday in Lent is the evangelist Mark's very brief account of the temptation of Christ. The temptation account may bring to your mind the movie, *The Last Temptation of Christ.* That movie gained much attention, because many people protested the substance of what was purported to be a possible last temptation of our Lord. The suggested temptation was that on the cross Jesus thought about what life would have been or might have been like had he loved a woman and married. Many Christians found it impossible to believe that Jesus would be open to the consideration of such notions. In reality, we do not know precisely how all the temptations did come to our Lord. However, we do know that our Lord "in every respect has been tempted as we are, yet without sin" (Hebrews 4:11). Therefore, he had to be tempted in regard to his sexuality also. Thus the movie achieved a notoriety it never should have and was not all that good for other reasons. All of that has been much discussed before.

What is important for us to understand is that Jesus was tempted all through his life, every day of his life. Of all of those temptations, the most troublesome ones had to be the kind of temptation he experienced in the very beginning of his ministry. Those temptations had to do with the use of power, and they were repeated in a variety of ways throughout his ministry. Though the Markan

17

account of our Lord's temptation appears very brief, it does include important observations which are most important for us to note.

Spirit-driven

The very first thing Mark records is that our Lord was involved in this encounter with Satan, because he was Spirit-driven. Mark relates his accounts in reportorial style. That style reveals a genuine sense of urgency, which is obvious in the temptation account. Jesus, according to Mark, had appeared on the scene when he came to be baptized by John. At his baptism Jesus had been anointed with the Spirit of God. Mark notes that was such a powerful experience, and the Spirit came upon Jesus with such force, that Jesus was immediately driven into the wilderness.

When Jesus uses the powers of his spirit to drive out demons from people, the same word is used that is employed by Mark to suggest that this was an irresistible power. This was no natural compulsion which people develop out of habit. This was the same dynamic influence as had been noted in the lives of God's people throughout their history. This Spirit was the force of God's presence in the lives of heroic people. It was the same Spirit God had conferred upon his creatures at the creation. In the life of Jesus, the Spirit of God was operating with full force and with its pristine power as God had intended God's Spirit should have been operative in people.

The Wilderness

The second observation Mark mentions is that "the Spirit immediately drove him (Jesus) out into the wilderness." The wilderness recalls that the Children of Israel were in the wilderness. However, that suggests two different kinds of experiences. On the one hand, the wilderness was the scene of God's revelation to his people. In the wilderness God had made a covenant with his people at Sinai. The wilderness was the place where God cared for and fed his people with manna. The wilderness was the land where God forged his people into a strong nation who could go up and take the Promised Land. At the same time, the wilderness was the scene of many open rebellions against God.

If the wilderness was thought of as a place to evoke faith and piety, it also brought out the worst in people and caused them to lose faith. For that reason alone the wilderness could be regarded as a place to be feared. If God was there, so were the wild beasts and all sorts of demons. The wilderness was the arena where one could sense dramatically the presence of both. The wilderness was a huge set where the desert storm of the battle of the godly and the demonic could take place. That is precisely why Jesus was driven by the Spirit into the wilderness. The battle lines had to be drawn between the one who thought he was holding sway in the world, the pretender to the throne of God, the Evil One, and the One who had come not only to challenge him but to empty him of his false powers.

The Forty Days

Mark cites the fact that Jesus was in the wilderness "forty days." More than likely, what comes to your mind is the fact that the Children of Israel were in the wilderness forty years. The forty days could, therefore, be reminiscent of those forty years and symbolic of that era of God's grace for God's people. However, what is probably more significant is the fact that Moses had been in Mount Sinai for forty days. Likewise, Elijah's flight from Jezebel lasted forty days when he went to Mount Horeb. In each of these cases these men of God emerged from their experience of solitude as greatly strengthened. Both Elijah and Moses came away with a clearer understanding of themselves and of what they were called to be and to do.

The forty days were not simply a rounded number made to conform to the number of years the Children of Israel had been in the making. The span of time mentioned is the time that it took God to prepare his holy men for the kind of mission God wanted them to perform. Jesus stood in their tradition. He was the young rabbi who had come to perform a prophetic role on behalf of God for the sake of God's people. Jesus had to know full well that when the Spirit drove him into the wilderness that he was stepping into the mediating roles of a Moses and the prophetic role of an Elijah. Jesus neither shirked these roles or protested them. It was the very nature of his Spirit to look at the experience as something that would help to prepare and mature him for what would follow.

Tempted

Mark reports quite simply, Jesus "was in the wilderness forty days, tempted by Satan." From the other evangelists we know that there were three major temptations. Mark's announcement is not just matter-of-fact stuff. The language he uses indicates the gravity of the situation. Also, its position in Mark's gospel makes it clear that all of this was a prelude to a ministry that actively countermanded the activities of the demonic. Nor should we assume that Mark knew of only one temptation. Rather, the reporting here is because he knows of only one, the struggle of our Lord for forty days. Having been commissioned by the Heavenly Father for his ministry, Jesus had to determine in what form he would carry out this ministry. Having received the approval of his Father, "This is my beloved Son," Jesus had to contemplate how he could best continue to please his Heavenly Father. It took the full forty days to think through and envision what kind of entanglements he was likely to face.

What would be the best way to show the understanding Jesus had of power? If he was the Son of God, would it not be appropriate for him to reverse what happened in the Garden of Eden by showing how he could make bread for the world? The first Adam had brought hardship to the world for the earning of one's bread, why not turn it all around by proving his sonship in making bread out of stones. Moses also fed the people in the wilderness. Why not prove your claim to being the second Moses? In the light of the best traditions in the Hebrew community, all of that sounded logical and beautiful. One can imagine how those thoughts tumbled over and over again in the mind of Jesus during those forty days. Everyone would know that Jesus of Nazareth was the greatest prophet there ever was.

Tempted More

The idea of being a great prophet had its appeal. Equally tempting had to be the idea that he was to be a priestly figure. The

Temple of Jerusalem, Herod's temple, represented the shrine where the people of God knew they could meet their God. That temple also represented the centuries of tradition, worship and culture of this people who knew their lives were uniquely bound up in a special pact between God and them. The sacrificial system of the ages had assured them of God's grace and love. Was it not for that reason the promised messianic figure should suddenly appear in the Temple? Would it not make good sense to drop into that scene like a bolt out of the blue so that the people could know that their great high priest had come? That certainly had to be an especially attractive scheme. That suggestion certainly had to twirl around in that great mind with great persistence.

Ah, but the most striking of all had to be the establishing a claim to David's throne! That would enable him to reinstate a reign more glorious, powerful, and victorious than Israel had ever known. With his know-how and abilities he could claim a place among the nations of the earth that would enable him to rule the world.

Our Temptations

If we can envision our Lord in the wilderness struggling with these immensely attractive ideas of the use of power in establishing himself as prophet, priest, and king, we will have some inkling as to how strikingly fascinating these notions were. In contrast, Jesus would have to think of being humiliated by the heartless people who would put him to death. If you understand that, you will also recognize the similarity to our own temptations. Temptations to the worst evils are charming and promising. A good businessman may have no problem resisting the temptation to embezzle, but if he ever had the opportunity to walk off with a million dollars, that might be difficult. People do tend to have their own price, one way or another.

All of us have to face the fact that temptations usually come tailored to fit our situations. They normally come on the heels of perfect rationalizations of why we should and could get away with something. We are willing to set aside what we know, our morals, and our best behavior to take up what we are sure will be for our benefit. Flip Wilson's famous line in *The Devil Made Me Do It* is to the lady contemplating the purchase of a dress she does not need is, "You owe yourself a try-on." That is where most temptation begins, "You owe yourself!" Then, of course, what follows is the "try-on" or "there's no harm in trying."

Beasts And Angels

Certainly as Jesus was bombarded with thoughts of glory and power, he had to wonder over and over again why the Heavenly Father would prefer him to go the way of suffering, pain, and the cross. If at the baptism God had claimed him as God's Son, why could he not think he could walk into the wild blue yonder with the world at his feet? Each one of us daily confronts the same kind of question one way or another. We lay claim to being God's children, and we are tempted to think that affords us special privileges, immunities, and rights. However, it does not work that way.

Mark says that while Jesus was in the wilderness "he was with the wild beasts; and the angels waited on him." In the Scriptures wild animals are sometimes described as a part of the kingdom of evil. What this suggests to us is that Jesus was hounded by temptation. At the same time the "angels waited on him." Those conditions were to be the same all the way to the cross. Jesus would be tempted on all sides, but God also sent his ministering angels to support him in resisting the evil. That is our comfort also. We would still have to be in doubt as to what the outcome would be, were it not for the fact that our Lord was victorious. For our sake he was victorious in the wilderness, all the way to the garden and on the cross itself. The Father awakened him from the grave as fully victorious. Now we can know that not only do angels attend us in our struggles in the wilderness of this world with the wild beasts, but we are already victorious in Christ and can resist temptation at every turn.

22

Take Up
Your Cross

Glenn Tinder, Professor of Political Science at the University of Massachusetts at Boston, has written a book titled, *The Political Meaning of Christianity.* While the author acknowledges that what he offers is an interpretation, he also believes that he represents a view that could be common to many Christians. He unabashedly confesses that he is beholden to a unique point of view. What he sees as different is that his stance is less optimistic than some Christian perspectives. This is not to say that the Christian operates without hope. However, the hope must be placed in God and not in people.

Pointedly, Tinder says that Christianity is consistently skeptical about political ideals and plans, because of what people are. Christianity must employ language and ideas that are not attractive to the world either. That could not be more explicit than it is stated by our Lord in the Holy Gospel for today. In this reading we hear Jesus predict his own passion. Peter tries to reject that notion. Jesus then not only rebukes him for that, but goes on to say that all his followers should be willing to take up their crosses. The language does not appear to be attractive when Jesus talks about self-denial, losing one's life, and being able to turn one's back on an "adulterous and sinful generation." If this is the nitty-gritty of our faith, where are we going to find people to make that kind of commitment? Jesus would reply that we had better do so, if we do not want to lose everything.

The Hard Facts

The reason that the disciples had a difficult time accepting the prediction of our Lord's passion is that they were basically selfish. That is the universal problem in the world. It should not be difficult in our day and age to point that out. Wars are waged in the world as the result of basic selfishness. The world economy is in tough straits because of human selfishness. The budget problems of our own nation are enormous in a land of unparalleled resources, because greed dictated policies and practices that are now a threat to our comfortable manner of living.

All nations are living in a profound state of confusion today. Economies everywhere are threatened, and everyone knows that the difficulties are linked to governing and political philosophies and practices. The evidence of human selfishness comes in massive doses. Tinder suggests that what the Holy Gospel for today suggests is something that all people have to take seriously. Whether they are Christian or not, or do not even want to consider becoming Christian, they should listen to what Christianity has to say. If we are to learn from political scientists and behaviorists, then certainly they should be open-minded to hear what Christianity has to say about human selfishness.

Deny Yourself

When you peel apart the saying of Jesus in the Holy Gospel for today you realize how devastating Jesus is in his evaluation of what we are and what humanity is. Jesus refused to be tempted by Peter to avoid the path to the cross. As Jesus had refused the temptations of Satan in the wilderness, he now dubs the protest of Peter as equally satanic, and tells him, "Get behind me, Satan! For you are not on the side of God but of men." Jesus does not hesitate to use the occasion to teach others. He gathers the people around him along with his disciples and says, "If any would come after me, let them deny themselves." Things are so bad that Jesus finds it necessary to tell us that we must cancel out ourselves. That

24

is not difficult to substantiate. History is not kind to the human enterprise.

When we get down to analyzing it all, with all of the best in human achievement, we realize that in the final analysis we cannot rely on humanity. The most idealistic revolutions carry in them the seeds of destruction. The finest of technological discovery and invention can be used against us. It is for this reason that Jesus calls us to deny ourselves lest we be caught up in our own weaknesses. It is a natural trait for us to try to overcome our own weaknesses, justify our own failures, and rationalize our behavior. Jesus calls us from all of that. That is what it means to deny ourselves. It is the call to give up on trying to make something of ourselves on our own. It is not that Jesus does not count us important or disdains us. The point is that Jesus wants to show us not only a better way, but the only way to genuinely affirm ourselves.

Take Up Your Cross

Jesus pushes the invitation to deny ourselves further. He encourages us to take up our cross and follow him. Jesus had informed the disciples what was ahead for him. He sensed that a cross awaited him. He knew that was a necessity. It was necessary, because God wanted to deal with what was creating havoc in all relationships, both human and divine. In Jesus, God came to the human situation that had been all fouled up. The humans whom God had created did not trust God and brought disaster in the form of death upon themselves, because to live outside God is to live outside the source of life.

God came on the scene to take that matter into his own hands. That meant death to God in order not only to bridge death, but to build the bridge to people. In dying upon the cross God demonstrated God's willingness to live in solidarity with the human race. Jesus took up the cross and in the resurrection made his cross a bridge to God and God's bridge to people. It is in the cross of our Lord Jesus Christ, then, that we find that we are a part of eternity. It is in our willingness to suffer whatever cross is laid on us with faith in the God who created us that we discover life. In dying we live. In suffering we make great gain. All of that, however, is implicit in our faith in God. Suffering or dying simply for the sake of suffering or dying nets us nothing. It is by faith in this gracious God that we transcend history, the problems of humanity, our own suffering, and our own death.

What Profit

On the surface of it, the sayings of Jesus appear harsh and impossible to follow. A common complaint against Christianity is that it is altogether too pessimistic about humanity, and all the talk about coping with suffering or being willing to suffer is just so much palaver. Jesus, however, actually puts it all into proper perspective. We are to follow Christ in the way of the cross, Jesus says, "For those who want to save their life will lose it, and those who lose their life for my sake, and for the sake of the Gospel, will save it. For what will it profit them to gain the whole world and forfeit their life? Indeed, what can they give in return for life?" In reality Jesus puts it right on the line. Jesus is the most pessimistic one can be about people trying to save their own situation. "What can they give in return for their life?" The answer is absolutely nothing! The case for humanity on its own is utterly hopeless.

On the other hand, Jesus also places the highest value on life. Jesus exalts life more than people can exalt it. Jesus pits the value of human beings against the wealth of the whole wide world. In the wilderness he had been tempted to use his powers to gain the whole world. However, that would have netted him nothing. All of that would have passed. The fate of humanity and of this world is to die. Jesus came to elevate humanity above the fate it deserved and earned and apparently courts and wants in its frantic efforts to save itself. But no matter how hard people try on their own they are bound to forfeit life. What Jesus announces and offers is that people do not have to suffer this fate. In him they can achieve a destiny that links them with eternity.

Guaranteed — No Loss

It is most obvious that what Jesus says is true when he says, "Those who want to save their life will lose it." We can all see that in many ways. The person who is the most industrious about trying to amass wealth has to leave it behind. The person who lives frantically, trying to get all of the pleasures out of life, may finally discover that he dies from just plain dissipation. The person who is the most diligent about health care must also finally surrender even after the most exotic surgery and most sophisticated electronic medicine have done their parts.

However, the person who comes to understand that life is something other than all of what we can do with our physical existence discovers that in the death and resurrection of our Lord Jesus Christ we become a part of eternity. We discover life when we find our lives wrapped in the death and resurrection of Jesus of Nazareth. In him our lives reach beyond the limitations of space and time. We are no longer fated for death. We are destined for eternity. Thus, when we lose the old life, we are losing our dependence upon ourselves to come up with a solution to the death that dogs us. We gain the life that is hidden in Christ, the life that exalts us beyond all human expectation and places an immeasurable value upon us.

Don't Misunderstand

The great difficulty with these sayings of Jesus is that they are so apt to be misunderstood, precisely, because people think they should use them to save themselves. Some people may shrug them off because they think they are too hard. Others are apt to think that they have to work hard to do them. They turn them into a morality play. They think they should deny themselves by giving up something. Or they think they should go out of their way to suffer or that they can use their suffering as a good work. All of that puts people in the same bind. On those terms they are once again trying to save themselves. What Jesus sees is just the opposite.

To put it in the most crass way — you know how often we have to say, "Don't just stand there. Do something!" However, in essence what Jesus says in the Gospel is, "Don't do anything. Just stand there!" That is what it means to deny ourselves rightly. The basic sin in the world is that the greatest inclination to evil is that

27

we want to exalt ourselves rather than to let God exalt us. This is what Tinder says so well. No matter what sin you are talking about it is the effort of the individual trying to control things and people around the self. To go the way of the cross with our Lord Jesus Christ is to discover that we do not have to do that. We are able to lose our lives and gain them in this Christ, because we do not have to earn, beg, borrow, or steal our self-worth. It is the given that comes from the God who proves that he loves us so much that he was willing to go to the cross for us.

No Shame

Jesus concludes his generous offer for us to find our lives by following him to the cross with an important observation. He says, "Those who are ashamed of me and of my words in this adulterous and sinful generation, of them the Son of Man will also be ashamed when he comes in the glory of his Father with the holy angels." This is not sour grapes. Jesus simply states the facts that should be most plain. Most surely international events of any given year should make it perfectly plain that we live in an adulterous and sinful generation. If you do not want to admit to that, then listen to the national news on your television tonight and judge whether you live in a sinful and adulterous generation or not. If that does not do it, watch the local news.

What Jesus is saying is that anyone who is foolish enough to take one's chances with a world that is so obviously fouled up and cannot learn from its own history deserves to fall with it. Why should we be ashamed of God's own Son who comes into the world to assure us of his Father's love and then lives it out by suffering and dying for us? That just does not make sense. The one sure thing you know about the world is that this Christ who died in this world and rose again will come again in all his glory with his holy angels. If we do not want to identify with that, then we will be stuck. He and the whole host of heaven will have to count it a shame that we ignored him. Far better for us to deny ourselves and take up the cross and follow him to glory.

Jesus
Transfigured

Dr. Jaroslav Pelikan of Yale University wrote a remarkable study of the significance of the person and work of Jesus Christ, *Jesus Through the Centuries*. Dr. Pelikan demonstrates how Jesus has been the dominant figure in the history of Western culture. Each age has made Jesus relevant to its own needs. Jesus has furnished each new age with answers to fundamental questions as every generation has had to address new social problems that tested the more fundamental questions of human existence. The world had to take note of Jesus as a rabbi, as the Cosmic Christ, the Ruler of the World, the King of Kings, the Prince of Peace, the Son of Man, the True Image of Man, the Great Liberator. In many other ways Jesus furnished the answers and the images that affected society in positive ways.

Dr. Pelikan's thesis is that Jesus did not and does not belong to the churches and the theologians alone, but that he belongs to the world. None of this is to say that we can make Jesus what we want Jesus to be. Quite the opposite. It is to say that the Christ is adequate for all our needs and that Jesus transcends culture in such a way that he is able to belong to each age and to address the issues of all time. To understand that, we can do no better than to look to the Holy Gospel for today, which celebrates the transfiguration of our Lord. In that momentous event we learn how and why Jesus belongs to the centuries.

The Event

We are not quite sure when this took place, though Mark tells us it was "after six days." That probably is a reference to a time after Peter had made his confession, "You are the Christ," when Jesus had asked the disciples who they thought he was. It was also at that occasion that Jesus informed the disciples that he would have to go up to Jerusalem and suffer and die, but that after three days he would rise again. It was then that Peter said that they would not permit this to happen, and Jesus said, "Get behind me, Satan." Jesus also said that this was God's will and that if any would follow him they would have to take up the cross and be willing to lose one's life in order to find it.

While we have a feeling that the transfiguration followed six days after the incident, we are sure that Mark wants to impress us with the fact that the glorious moment on the mount was the prelude to our Lord's great passion. What transpired in the mount was a beginning for those events that would reach their climax in the death of Christ. For this reason we note that Mark refers to the six days as comparable to the six days when Moses prepared himself to climb Mount Sinai to meet God when Moses was glorified.

The Happening

One certainly cannot read the gospel accounts of the transfiguration of our Lord without thinking of the parallel to the account of Moses on Mount Sinai. Just as Jesus is transfigured in this brilliant display of light that made him into a dazzling sight, who should appear but Moses himself along with the prophet Elijah. Both of the legendary figures had been assumed into heaven after they had completed long and faithful careers as prophets. It was obvious that they are a part of the company of heaven who live in the presence of God. What was more important is that their ministries had been filled with the same kind of torment, temptation and persecution as had been crammed into the ministry of our Lord. No other prophets had also suffered so much faithlessness and testing from the very people whom they had served so faithfully.

God could not have sent better representatives to talk with Jesus. They were the experienced veterans who could talk about what they had encountered. And talk they did. Mark records simply that they "were talking with Jesus." The evangelist Luke is the one who tells us that they talked about "his departure which he was to accomplish at Jerusalem" (Luke 9:31). They were preparing Jesus for what he still had to face. The worst was yet to come. However, no doubt, they also could assure Jesus that God would see him through death all the way through the tomb via the resurrection. What capped that comforting counsel was the voice that came out of a cloud that overshadowed them, "This is my Son the Beloved; listen to him!" Then suddenly it was all over. The disciples "saw no one with them any more, but only Jesus."

A Reaction

The whole effect was so startling for the three disciples, Peter, James, and John, that they were frightened. They were not simply stunned, but Mark says they "were terrified." They were party to an extraordinary religious experience. The cloud that had overshadowed them was the same as the *shekinah*, the cloud that had traversed with the children of Israel as a sign of God's presence. It was also as the cloud that enveloped Mount Sinai when Moses went up to be the mediator for the people.

The disciples behaved no differently than the children of Israel who had been frightened by the scene at Sinai. It was as though Peter had been carried back to that scene in time so that he should suggest that they make three booths, one for Jesus, one for Moses, and one for Elijah. Certainly, booths would not suggest permanent memorials like shrines or temples. Booths would be reminiscent of the booths the children of Israel built in the wilderness. Or booths would also recall the tent of the tabernacle which had been the place of worship in the wilderness. What is notable is that Peter indicates he puts Jesus in a scene that would be comfortable for all three, and that impermanent shelters suggest that he knows the scene must move on.

Some Gibberish

What Peter suggested was the best that he could think of at the moment. The disciples were next to being speechless. This was unlike the many marvelous signs that they had witnessed Jesus perform. This was something done for him and to him. Their fear was not unlike that of the children of Israel at Sinai. Sinners who stand in the presence of the holy and righteous God run for some kind of cover. Peter tried to make the most of the moment by trying to prolong it. Even temporary shelters could house these sacred people for a time. They could decide later how to continue with this remarkable experience. Whatever Peter had in mind, we can identify with the way a person who is taken by surprise is astonished and frightened at the same time can come up with some form of gibberish. Yet what is obvious is that Peter felt a compulsion to try to do something with Jesus.

As usual, Peter was the one to make a bold suggestion. And as he was wont to do, Peter thought that he could make the most of the situation by suggesting how Jesus could preserve the best of the scene. As earlier Peter has mentioned that Jesus should put the cross out of his mind, here he thinks that Jesus should try to stay in the mountain and prolong what was happening in this glorious sight. This was as good a place as any to hide out and away from the threat down below in the city. Up here in the mountain they could spend their time in useful prayer and devotion.

It Was Not To Be

However, Peter's brilliant idea of what could have been a good way to continue to the joy of that moment was not to be. Moses and Elijah had come to discuss the unfinished business that lay ahead of Jesus. The voice that spoke the benediction from heaven was also clear on the matter. While that special word which had to be of great consolation and inspiration to Jesus also gave special instruction to the witnesses to this marvelous happening, "This is my beloved Son; listen to him." Peter, James, and John were exhorted to pay attention to what Jesus had to say and what he would do.

No sooner had that voice faded, when the disciples could see no one "but Jesus only" then, "as they were coming down the mountain, he (Jesus) charged them to tell no one what they had seen, until the Son of man should have risen from the dead." The disciples were to listen to that, but they did not pay very good attention. One would have expected that they would have engaged Jesus in some meaningful dialogue about the resurrection from the dead and how he would accomplish that. One would think that they would have been excited about that kind of news, because Jesus was claiming that he would be able to defeat the worst enemy of all, death. But there absolutely were no indications at all that these three disciples understood them or remembered when Jesus was crucified that he had promised to rise from the dead.

Our View

We cannot be too hard on the disciples for not getting the full import of what had taken place before them and how Jesus had instructed them. If we had been there we would have reacted the same way. Probably most of us would not have been able to think of one thing to say. We would have been numb and speechless like James and John. It would have been strange indeed if any of us looked forward to suffering. We think those people are sick who find delight in suffering. We all do what we can to avoid suffering. Peter was saying what we all think, "Who needs the cross? Let's remain where it is safe and we can pray and avoid all the trouble." Besides who can understand the resurrection? No doubt you have read in newspapers, books, and journals that people believe in the immortality of the soul. Who needs the resurrection?

We do not like to believe that Jesus had to leave that most beautiful scene of glorification to come down into the world of sin and death and die for us sinners. We do not like to believe that the only way possible for God to make it clear and plain to us that we should die for our sins was to have Jesus die for us. The only way that God could make it plain to us that God is willing to forgive our sins and share eternity with us was to raise Jesus from the dead and promise that God would do the same for us. It is apparent from this story, however, that as plainly as Jesus did tell that to the disciples at that moment they did not believe it. And we have to admit that we all struggle with the truth of it also.

Our Hope

However, in spite of our struggles like those of the disciples, Jesus did accomplish what he said he would. The transfiguration event was not what Peter wanted to make of it. This was God's special moment for the strengthening of this unique Son to prepare Jesus for the cross and the resurrection. By so doing, Jesus completed the work that far transcended what Peter would have made of Jesus. Jesus "abolished death and brought life and immortality to light through the gospel" (2 Timothy 1:10). This is why Dr. Pelikan could demonstrate that Jesus belonged to the centuries.

Jesus was not one who belonged to one age, one movement, one revolution, or one phase of history that was soon to pass. The one who dealt with the reality of our sin and judgment and gave us life and hope by the resurrection from the dead is the One who furnishes us with the forgiveness, the freedom, and the hope for dealing with all the ills that confront us. Our Lord's moment of glory in the mountain was to prepare him for the hours of agony and suffering in his passion that he might win eternity for us. From him we gain the strength to work, to suffer, and to die in the sure and certain hope of eternity.

Clean House

The portrait of our Lord Jesus Christ in the Holy Gospel appointed for this day has proven to be something of a conundrum for interpreters through the years. What we see is the Lord Jesus in a violent rage driving animals and people out of the Temple. Years ago Bruce Barton, in a very popular book, *The Man Nobody Knows,* used the story to demonstrate how virile the Lord Jesus was. He surmised that the Lord Jesus was capable of herculean strength and prowess because of his outdoorsy lifestyle and vigorous walking missionary tours. However, others have been concerned that this public demonstration which had all the earmarks of a near riot was most unbecoming of the normal life style of Jesus. Also, if this were a pique of temper, could not someone accuse Jesus of being guilty of a sin which all of us dislike very much?

Then, of course, there is the additional problem of finding this story in the beginning of the Fourth Gospel, whereas the other evangelists place it in Holy Week at the beginning of his passion. Could it be true that Jesus cleansed the Temple twice? Is John right and the others wrong? Or is it the other way around? Or could there be another reason why John places the story where he does? There is good reason to think that it is the latter. The story of Jesus cleansing the Temple helps us to understand several very important aspects of the church and its worship.

The Context

The evangelist relates for us that this occasion was a Passover festival. The Passover attracted worshippers to Jerusalem from all over the world. They came speaking different languages and carrying foreign monies. Enterprising merchants had set up booths and stalls in the Temple to accommodate the travelers coming to worship who needed to exchange their monies in order to pay their temple taxes and make their contributions. Others were busy selling animals to be used in the sacrifices. To be sure, there was great commotion and excitement. One can imagine the carnival character of those festal days as travelers found relatives and old friends among the many consumers who populated the precincts of the Temple.

The temple area covered some 35 acres. It had originally been built by Solomon about 950 B.C., but was burned to the ground by Nebuchadnezzar in 587 B.C. The Temple was rebuilt under Zerubbabel in 516 B.C. It was desecrated and stripped by Antiochus Epiphanes in 168 B.C. and cleansed and restored by Judas Maccabaeus in 165 B.C. The temple in which Jesus found himself amid these cattlemen and money sharks was the glorious temple begun by Herod the Great, who began the work in 20 B.C. It was not yet completed while Jesus was there and was not finished until 68 A.D., a short time before its complete destruction in 70 A.D. The Herodian Temple was extremely lavish and more beautiful than the Temple of Solomon.

The Importance

With this long history of the Temple in the life of the Hebrew people, one can imagine how important a shrine this was. From the very beginning of the Hebrew people, sacred places had been important to the patriarchs. Then, the tabernacle, the traveling shrine of a tent, had been the center of the life of the Hebrew community. However, just as the people longed for a monarchy with a throne as other peoples had, they wanted a permanent shrine. The most popular of all their kings, David, gathered the materials for his son Solomon to build the first temple on that holy site, Mount Moriah, where Abraham had offered to sacrifice his son

Isaac. The temple had always symbolized for the people the presence of their most holy God, Jahweh. That is why it was so important that after each time the Temple was destroyed that it be restored to proclaim once again the assured presence of the Almighty and Holy One of Israel.

It was especially gratifying for the people that Herod the Great should have given so much attention to the restoration of the Temple in such an extravagant manner. Herod had done much to promote the hellenistic or Greek culture with special buildings. However, he also curried the favor of the Jews by investing so much in the building of their shrine. The people were grateful to worship in Herod's temple, regardless of Herod's motives. The temple was the center of their life and helped to define what it meant to be a Jew. It gave shape and form not only to the Hebrew worship but also to their entire culture.

The Shock

Recognizing the centrality of the Temple, and the joyous character of that festal moment, you can imagine what kind of shock waves ran through the Temple and the entire city of Jerusalem when this controversial rabbi created the ruckus he did in the temple area! It appears this happened at the beginning of the feast when the greatest excitement had to do with the preparations so that the commerce had to be at its height. Into that busy crowd Jesus rushed with a homemade whip of cords and struck out wildly at people and animals to put them into a rout.

The reason that the Evangelist John includes this story at the very beginning of his gospel is because he wants to show throughout his gospel that Jesus gave new shape and meaning to the worship life of the people of God. In this very early story John is able to set the stage for all that is to follow in explaining the sacramental character of the worship life of the church. Therefore it is quite striking when Jesus shouts as he confronts those selling the little doves for sacrifice, "Take these things out of here! Stop making my Father's house a marketplace!" Jesus had come to replace the sacrificial system of the Hebrew covenant, by making the once-for-all sacrifice on a cross.

Quite symbolically, Jesus was driving out the old system. However, at the same time he was making it clear that he was highly displeased that people had made their sacrifices and their worship commercial.

A Sign, Please!

The disciples were really shaken by what they witnessed Jesus doing. This does not appear to be the same Jesus who is so gentle and considerate otherwise. However, the evangelists said that they "remembered that it was written, 'Zeal for your house will consume me.'" They recalled Psalm 69 which they saw Jesus fulfill. They understood at that moment Jesus was making a rightful claim to his Father's house. That meant he clearly identified himself as God's Son, who was linked to all that God had revealed in the covenant read in the First Lesson this morning. That covenant established God's claim on the undivided attention, affection, and trust of this people. Just so, Jesus forcefully demonstrated his right to claim the fidelity of this people.

The people were impressed, taken back, but quizzical. "What sign can you show us for doing this?" they asked. Jesus answered, "Destroy this temple, and in three days I will raise it up." That sent the people reeling. They responded. "This temple has been under construction for 46 years, and will you raise it up in three days?" The Herods had been at it all this time and it was still not finished, and Jesus thought he could rebuild it in three days! That was ridiculous. This Jesus of Nazareth was impossible. The disciples were also confused at this time. They did not understand. The evangelist says that "after he was raised from the dead, his disciples remembered that he had said this; and they believed the scripture and the word that Jesus had spoken."

The Body Of The Church

It was in the light of the death and resurrection of our Lord Jesus Christ that we can understand this spectacular event. As John had placed this event at the beginning of his gospel to indicate how Jesus had come to replace the former manner of worship with the sacramental life of the church, he was also saying something about the nature of the church. Formerly, the people of God had to be reassured of the presence of God by symbols and the people had to gather at shrines symbolized by the likes of the Temple; now they would gain those assurances in Christ himself.

The assurance of God's presence among us is the Risen Christ. Jesus died for our sins and rose again that he might be present among us. Because this Risen Christ is present among us in the Spirit of God given to us, the Apostle Paul could refer to us as the Body of Christ. The Church is the Body of Christ. Thus it was true that the people did destroy the Body of Christ, but he was raised to new life in three days, and we are now part of that Body. The boast that Jesus made that day in view of the promises of God and in perfect trust that God would complete them in him are now fulfilled in us.

The Sacramental Body

What was also important to the evangelist was the sacramental character of the church. When our Lord talked about the temple of his body replacing the Temple at Jerusalem, that was also true in a sacramental sense. The sacrificial system that was practiced in the Temple at Jerusalem along with the priestly entrance into the Holy of Holies were signs of God's grace and mercy for God's people. The people did not have to sacrifice themselves and they were always reminded of God's presence and their access to him. Now it is the Risen Christ who offers his body to us in the Holy Eucharist as the sure sign that he has been sacrificed for us and is present with us. In the giving of that body and blood to us we are literally filled with the Presence of the Risen Christ. Together we are his body.

Luther found it fascinating to talk about us as being baked into one loaf. As we all receive of the same bread and eat of the same together, we become one loaf. We are bonded together in this Christ. For us that means that we are not alone. Not only is God present in us, but we are also present in one another to be a strength and a presence for one another. We emphasize that when we go to the home of shut-ins bearing bread and wine that have been

39

consecrated in the Eucharist. For those who have not been present with us, Christ is present with them in the Sacrament, so we also are united with them in this body of Christ.

Our Worship

Later in his gospel John gives an account of a confrontation between Jesus and a woman of Samaria. When the woman perceived that Jesus was a prophet she asked him why the difference in attitude of the Samaritans and the Jews, who each claimed separate shrines for worshipping God. Jesus said to her, "The hour is coming and now is, when the true worshippers will worship the Father in spirit and truth, for such the Father seeks to worship him. God is Spirit, and those who worship him must worship him in spirit and truth" (John 4:23.24).

Taken with the Holy Gospel for this day we should understand that we can never permit buildings, symbols, signs, organizations, traditions, customs, liturgies, or any features of church life or worship to become substitutes for our real devotion to our Lord himself. All these things in themselves can become too important. We know how difficult it is to introduce a new book of worship, a new liturgy, a new hymn, or a new custom into the church, because people make idols of their traditions. Ask church officials also how difficult it is to close down a church building where only a handful still come to worship. When we worship God in spirit and in truth we know his Real Presence in us and among us is the Risen Christ, who is our Real Temple, our Real Altar. We worship him and adore him when we receive all that he offers to us by grace. We dramatize that when we come together for worship, and we gather him to ourselves when in faith we receive him.

Hate Evil

In the Holy Gospel appointed for today our Lord refers to the manner in which Moses "lifted up the serpent in the wilderness." The incident to which our Lord referred is narrated in the First Lesson. The occasion was the outburst of frustration when the Children of Israel had to backtrack from Mount Hor down to the Sea of Reeds to detour around Edom. The reason for the runaround was that the Edomites would not grant the Israelites a permit to pass through their land. Consequently, as the Israelites started their dreary march back into the desert, they started to moan and complain. They complained against both God and Moses for having brought them out of the security of their bondage in Egypt. Sometimes slavery and the lack of freedom can be far more safe and secure than freedom. So it was that the Israelites deemed that new freedom laid more burdens upon them than their past slavery in the Land of Pharaoh.

What was at stake, however, was the fact that the Israelites were questioning the divine providence and guidance of the God who had saved and redeemed them. They had contested the manner in which God was dealing with them. As is so common, their memories were not of the outstanding deliverance God had performed for them. It was for this reason that God permitted them to be attacked by the poisonous serpents whose bite was fatal.

That drove the people to their senses. They repented of their grumbling and rebellion against God and Moses. Moses interceded on their behalf. God heard the prayer and instructed Moses to prepare a brazen serpent upon which the people could look and be saved.

The Same Condition

The reason that Jesus saw a parallel between his own passion and the lifting up of the brazen serpent was because the conditions were the same. Whether it was Jesus who said it, or the evangelist who editorialized about it, the fact is that "God so loved the world that he gave his only Son so that everyone who believes in him may not perish but may have eternal life." The problem is that the world is perishing as surely as the Israelites were dying of poisonous venom. That is not difficult to see.

Yet we are stuck with the hard fact that at the end of this twentieth century nations still go to war. We know that we have to spend enormous sums to maintain a defense posture. Yet we have not found ways to make it just as emergent to fight the enemies of hunger, famine, and injustice the world over. The crises we face in the world are signs of how the world perishes. The world sows the seeds of its own destruction. Evil and demonic leadership highlight for us how people prefer to live in the bondage to their own desires rather than to live for the sake of others.

In the Dark

Another condition which is the same as that of the time of the children of Israel in the desert is that the world is in the dark. The evangelist says, "The people loved darkness rather than light." That was the same way in which the Israelites said they preferred the days of slavery in Egypt to the freedom under God in the desert. In the same way the world is in the dark today. There is all kind of evidence to support that also. There was a time when the great thinkers of the world, the philosophers, struggled with the great questions concerning life. The philosophers of the past wrestled with questions about God and the nature of people. Today that exercise of stretching the mind to try to touch God is over.

Philosophers have declared bankruptcy on that score. They simply feel that the questions concerning phenomena outside of scientific experience are out of bounds for them. They are right.

We cannot learn about God apart from what God tells or teaches us about himself. However, God has not left himself without witness. God has revealed himself. Therefore, those who cannot see in the light of this witness are in the dark. The world is very much in the dark and cannot find solutions to its own great problems. The behaviorists have to keep altering their findings and the human behavior changes. The sociologists have to keep revising their materials as the great social problems not only go unsolved but get larger and larger. The world is living in the dark. And the real tragedy, the evangelist reports, is that the "people loved darkness rather than light." The proof of that again is: just remember all the times when some crusader tries to bring about a social reform only to discover how much the world prefers its darkness.

Evil Deeds

Because people of the world "loved darkness rather than light, their deeds were evil." Sin is so obvious in the world that one does not have to advance much of an argument to show that people are capable of great evil. Broadcasts of atrocities have been so horrendous at times that they had to be cut because they had been so offensive to public viewing. As a daily log on human behavior, the newspaper gives us case history after case history of the evil deeds of people. Those are the obvious and glaring forms of evil deeds. However, that is not all that is meant here.

The evangelist explains his understanding of the deeds that are evil. He says, "All who do evil hate the light and do not come to the light, so that their deeds may not be exposed." This would include all the deeds that people do that may be ever so acceptable and even laudable but which cannot be exposed because of their motivation. The person who does good service but does it for one's own selfish reasons or benefits is evil. All of the manipulating, the self-serving, and the selfish behavior of people is evil. No matter how pious or how religious people may sound in the doing of that which is aimed at elevating oneself, it is evil.

The Analogy

Because the condition of the world is so perishable that it can produce only evil deeds in its darkened condition, only God could rescue it. God did that in the sending of our Lord Jesus Christ. The analogy of why God had to do so is expressed by the brazen serpent that Moses lifted in the wilderness. The imminent threat of death present in those poisonous snakes that infiltrated the camp of the Israelites was a powerful motivation for the people to repent of their sins of unbelief and complaint in the desert. God could have used their helplessness as a time to extract from them promises that they would change their lives, clean up their acts and take loyalty oaths and make commitments never to sin against God again. However, that would not work.

If people were motivated only by fear and self-interest, the problem would persist. No matter how eager the people would be for change and protection, the motivations would still be from the same old self. The people would have to look outside themselves for the help. God dramatized that for the people by having Moses make a model of the very thing that was destroying them. However, this was one created by God for their salvation. The bronze snake became the sign of God's love and grace for the people. The people could look to the snake and be spared, because they trusted a word and promise from God. God made no bargain with the people. Rather, God gave the people the opportunity to test God's goodness, grace and mercy.

Judgment Withheld

The analogy of the brazen serpent lifted up by Moses in the wilderness is made by the evangelist as to how God had to lift up our Lord Jesus Christ. "So," he says, "must the Son of Man be lifted up, that whoever believes in him may have eternal life." The Son of Man was "lifted up" upon the cross and again when he ascended into heaven. The same Greek expression is used for both the crucifixion and the ascension. God had to allow his own Son

44

to be lifted up on the cross for the salvation of the world for the same reasons he had to provide the brazen serpent.

The world should have learned by now that it cannot believe in itself. Nothing in the world is trustworthy. Even our best friends let us down. That is just the way it is. But God is perfectly willing to sweep all that aside. "Indeed," says the evangelist, "God did not send his Son into the world to condemn the world, but in order that the world might be saved through him." God's love for the world is so great that he is perfectly willing to cover the situation for us. God provides the way out of our perishable, darkened and futile life by giving us the opportunity to trust him again. It is as plain and simple as that. "Those who believe in him are not condemned; but those who do not believe are condemned already, because they have not believed in the name of the only Son of God."

God Gives The Light

The unfortunate situation is that the dreadful state of humankind is not something God introduced. God does not have to judge the world, because the world has already judged itself. The world has brought about its own ruin, because of its failure to believe God. The first sin started that way, and the problem has been compounded beyond description. We were among those already condemned. However, as God gives us opportunity to find God trustworthy through our Lord Jesus Christ, we are spared the condemnation, because God never intended that we should be condemned. God never wanted people to be cut off from the fullness of God's love. In the Lord Jesus Christ we learn that about God. We learn that God was all love to begin with. We learn the truth about ourselves, and that we can afford to give up trying to make it on our own.

God has shined the light on the whole situation. The evangelist says, "Those who do what is true come to the light, so that it may be clearly seen that their deeds have been done in God." God gives us the light to see ourselves as we truly are, to see the fullness of his love and the richness of his grace. Then, to top it all off, we can clearly see that our "deeds have been done in God." That means that our entire lives have been filled with the righteousness of Christ. This is to say, that when we live by faith in this gracious God that God looks upon all that we do as having been redeemed and sanctified in Christ.

Live By Faith

How does this work? One explanation can be found in the business world. We are used to hearing about takeovers and buyouts. We hear about them both ways. We hear about the good ones and the bad ones. Sometimes a failing corporation may be taken over by another that is not that much better, and both of them go under. They share their weaknesses and both are lost. On the other hand, a good strong company may take over one with great weakness, bad debts and the like. In that case the weaker company benefits from the power and strength of the other. So it is with what our text has been telling us. The world that is already condemned can find no help in the world that is already condemned. However, our holy and righteous God has taken us over, bad debts and all, and we are the beneficiaries of all of God's righteousness. All that we are and have been is furnished with the righteousness of Christ.

In the Second Lesson this morning we hear it stated well, "By grace you have been saved through faith, and this is not your own doing; it is the gift of God ... not the result of works, so that no one may boast. For we are what he has made us, created in Christ Jesus for good works, which God prepared beforehand to be our way of life." All of that should give us encouragement. We should be able to discern what evil in the world truly is. Evil is not believing God. It is unbelief that we must hate. To cultivate goodness is to believe God and to trust that God does not condemn us. If we do that, we can count on God to do the rest. He will give us opportunity to do good and then count it righteous. No questions asked.

Which Way
To Jesus?

Great commotion was created in the holy city of Jerusalem at the time of the Feast of the Passover. On that occasion worshippers came from all over the Mediterranean world to fulfill their obligations at the Temple. A carnival atmosphere filled the precincts of the Temple with the commercial traffic that was created with the sale of animals for sacrifice and the exchange of foreign currency. Today the Holy Gospel takes us to the city during the festival. We are not in the court of the Temple but somewhere out in the city which is not only crowded but bubbling with the excitement that Jesus had created when he entered the city with his entourage.

The previous Sunday the people had given Jesus a stirring welcome and applauded him with the kind of acclamation normally reserved for a king. The excitement put a glow on the city and the company of Jesus in particular. The city had undoubtedly better than doubled its population with all the visitors. Crowded in and among them were the followers of Jesus who must have also grown in number as Jesus received the ovation and outstanding recognition on Sunday. No doubt anyone who had claimed any association with Jesus now wanted to be a part of his scene. Well, there were other people, too, who wanted to meet Jesus. It is their experience with Jesus that is worthy of our attention.

The Greeks

In the crowds pressing to get to Jesus, John says, were some Greeks. It is a good guess to say that these were people from Greece who were proselytes. That means they were Gentiles who had espoused the Hebrew faith and had come to observe the Feast of the Passover. They were not Hebrews who spoke Greek. However, they did have the good sense to seek out a disciple of Jesus, who had a Greek name and who came from a region where the Hebrews did speak Greek. We all know how that works. Quite commonly we say, "It's not what you know. It's who you know." That is true whether you are looking for a job, trying to get tickets to the Final Four, or trying to meet the guest soloist backstage at the symphony.

The Greeks went to someone who could understand them and probably would also be sympathetic to them. Philip responded to that well enough. Though he wanted to do something for the strangers, he was rather timid himself. He went to get another Greek-speaking disciple by the name of Andrew, and the two of them were able to usher the Greeks into the presence of Jesus. That is a good model for us, also. When one feels too timid to introduce someone to Jesus, it is a good idea to bring someone else along to help one over the rough spots. The timid person will feel more comfortable in the presence of someone who can serve as an alter ego.

We Wish To See Jesus

The Greeks who approached the disciple made the request in a polite form: "Sir, we wish to see Jesus." The substance of their request was that they wanted an interview with Jesus. They were not autograph hunters. They wanted to know about this Jesus. Undoubtedly their curiosity had been raised by the commotion about Jesus the previous Sunday. We have no idea of what they really expected to see or hear from Jesus. If they were like King Herod, who later had the chance for an interview with Jesus, they would want Jesus to perform some spectacular signs. People today come pursuing Jesus for different reasons.

The people's agendas are not all the same. Some people look to Jesus to be only a healer. Some want him to be the perfect shrink, a good psychiatrist or psychologist. Others want him to be the Great Reformer, the one who can cure all the ills of society. Still others want him to be the one to guarantee success as a Chief Executive Officer, who knows how to encourage people to achieve excellence. Still others are sure that Jesus can be the one to guarantee wealth, that to live life abundantly as Jesus said is to have a life of abundance filled with all good things. Then, of course, what was most likely in the excitement of the week in which the Greeks came was that people expected Jesus to be the perfect political leader, king, tzar, president or whatever it would take to make the ideal government.

Surprise

When the request of the Greeks was presented to Jesus, Jesus did not refuse to see the people. However, what he did say had to be a shock. Jesus used the occasion to make a most serious and solemn announcement. If these people wanted to see him, they would have to understand what was involved. He said, "The hour has come for the Son of Man to be glorified. Very truly, I tell you, unless a grain of wheat falls into the earth and dies, it remains a single grain; but if it dies, it bears much fruit. Those who love their life will lose it, and those who hate their life in this world will keep it for eternal life." That was not a very good prospect for these people who wanted to follow Jesus.

Jesus was headed for the cross, and he knew it. It was a moment he had been preparing for. This was zero hour. It was necessary. It could not be avoided. Jesus used the analogy of the grain of wheat that must die in the earth to illustrate that he must die and be buried for the sake of humankind. The point for the people who wanted to follow is that they should also be willing to die. They have to put to death their own sinful lives. Jesus called that "their life in this world." By that he meant the life that is attached to this world, that conceives of the good of this world as being the essence of life. If we love that life, we will be sure to lose it in death. However, if we are willing to put that life to death in Christ then we will keep life. That is not a contradiction. It involves a turning away from serving ourselves to following our Lord Jesus Christ.

How You Die

We, of course, know how Jesus died. In these Lenten days we meditate upon the Passion and death of our Lord, who was crucified as a common criminal. Accused both by religious and civil communities, he died an ignominious death as an insurrectionist and blasphemer. Both crimes were the highest offense against either the state or the church. We know that Jesus was guilty of neither. Yet that is not what the law said. Under the law he died as accused. We know that it was for our sake that he willingly submitted to this treatment under the law of God. But now how do we follow him into death? We all know we are going to die some day. But how do we die the kind of death of which Jesus speaks? Jesus made that possible.

In baptism we already have experienced our own funeral. In baptism we have been put to death with Christ, and as all our sins were nailed to the cross with Christ, so they were buried with Christ. Each time we say the Lord's prayer or hear the absolution we recall the funeral of our old nature. Each time we come to the sacrament of the altar we die to sin again. Christ makes it possible to follow him into death through the Gospel and the Sacraments. In so doing we can leave behind the old self every day, and every day begin anew in him. In so doing we can live as those who can live above the world and live in him by faith, which is to live eternally, beginning right now.

The Glory Of It

When Jesus spoke of these prospects, however, things did not look all that good. Here come these strangers, who certainly must have appeared to flatter Jesus by taking the time to look him up and express their interest. Then Jesus comes back with this very sober appraisal of his prospects. He is going to die, and asks his followers to die with him. However, Jesus called it his "hour of glory." Way back at the wedding of Cana he had told his mother his hour had not yet come (2:4). He said the same thing to his brother (7:8).

50

To be sure Jesus recognized this hour for what it was. It was trouble, and he said so publicly: "Now my soul is troubled. And what should I say — 'Father, save me from this hour?' " Later we know that he did suffer agony in the garden because of his impending trial and crucifixion, and the epistle for today speaks of his "prayers and supplications, with loud cries and tears." Yet in spite of what was ahead, Jesus would not try to escape. He confessed that this is why he had come. Consequently, Jesus prayed, "Father, glorify your name." Jesus had come to personify the very glory of God in what was to happen when he died upon the cross. It is in that ugly, dark, terrible moment when all the earth trembled and shook at the prospect of God's Son dying upon the cross that the glory of God was revealed. What was revealed was God's love. God in the flesh was dying for sinners. Paul says in that pitiful moment of weakness God showed his power (1 Corinthians 1:18). It is at the cross of Christ you touch God's glory and his power.

For Your Sake

John records that when Jesus spoke his brief prayer a voice came from heaven, "I have glorified it (my name), and I will glorify it again." What the voice meant was that God had revealed his glory in the creation of the first Adam. That had been spoiled by sin. Now God would glorify it again and restore innocency to the world through our Lord Jesus. The people did not know what they heard. Some thought it was thunder. Others thought an angel spoke to him. Jesus said that the voice had come for the sake of the people. Jesus already knew the glory of the Father. Now, however, through the Lord Jesus the people would be glorified. In what was happening, the climax of events that would transpire at the cross, Jesus said, "Now is the judgment of this world; now the ruler of this world will be driven out."

It would be obvious in the death of our Lord just how the unbelief of the world can result in the cruelty of killing the holy, innocent Son of God. That is the judgment of this world. It had judged and condemned itself. The death Jesus dies is the death it deserves. Because of that the devil is rendered virtually powerless.

51

The demons are driven out of the world of the people who recognize what God has done in both judging and saving the world. Thus, Jesus says, "And I, when I am lifted up from the earth, will draw all people to myself." Jesus' being lifted up, of course, was his description of the cross, but for John it also meant his being raised from the dead and ascended to heaven. That is why the voice and all that Jesus had spoken was for our sake. It was for the sake of the world. What Jesus accomplished was satisfaction for the sins of the whole world that all could be saved.

Serve Him

One note that Jesus also spoke for the benefit of the Greeks was, "Whoever serves me must follow me, and where I am there will my servant be also. Whoever serves me, the Father will honor." Jesus would have his way with us. All that Jesus summarized in his statement to his disciples for the benefit of the Greeks was realistic about what would transpire in his life. It was also realistic about what has to happen in our lives. However, the benefits are all ours.

If following Jesus appears difficult because we think we have something in ourselves or the world that we cannot give up, Jesus says we are bound to lose it. Following him through the cross, however, not only guarantees that we have eternal life, but we also live in the presence of Christ. Christ is present with us now. He gives the signs of that in the sacraments and pledges it in his Gospel. However, we also know that finally when we depart this world we will also be with him where he is. In addition to that Jesus says, "Whoever serves me, the Father will honor." Grandmothers used to say if you did something unselfishly you "would get stars in your crown." Better yet, serving our Lord in faith is guarantee that God will honor us right along with God's Son, and we shall be with him and like him.

The Sponge
And Wine

Our age has been called a drug culture. Offhand, it would be impossible to estimate the amount of drug abuse in our society. At times we believe that our intense efforts and huge expenditures to curtail drug abuse are successful only to discover otherwise. However, today we are also engaged in a national debate about the medicinal use of drugs as an important part of the health care delivery system. The drug industry is under scrutiny, because of the high cost of the society's reliance upon their products. The drug companies reply that their part in the national bill for health care is fair enough. Meanwhile, a significant portion of monies paid out for drugs is not curative but for the relief of pain.

Daily the populace consumes huge doses of aspirin, barbiturates, ibuprofen, and sedatives in order to get through a normal day. Patients in hospitals are able to administer sedation to themselves intravenously. Those dying in hospices and intensive care wards are sedated sufficiently to make them immune to the pain that signals their imminent death. We applaud these advances in medicine that are capable of relieving the painful distress of patients at any level. Because of our approval of those efforts, we should be all the more sensitive to the manner in which the evangelists relate that attention that was given to sedate our Lord for his crucifixion.

A Routine Courtesy

While the evangelists give us some details concerning the passion of our Lord, more than any other portion of his mission and ministry, by today's standards we have sparse information. What we do have, then, is all the more important. The fact that each evangelist mentions something about the sedation of Jesus at the cross is highly significant. To begin with, we note that Mark mentions the attempt of the soldiers to sedate Jesus when they arrived at Golgotha.

As was customary, Jesus had been forced to carry the beam of his own cross. Jesus had been exhausted before that grueling march had begun. He had endured a dreadful scourging, the mockery of the soldiers, and night examination by the courts. Under those conditions, it was no surprise that Jesus would stagger under the load of the cross, or that a Roman soldier had only to tap an innocent bystanding citizen with his spear to substitute for Jesus. After all, it was an occupied country. At the cross the soldiers followed the usual routine for crucifixion, which also included offering a drink of drugged wine in order to deaden the pain. A group of wealthy women from Jerusalem apparently made this potion as a project of mercy for citizens who had to suffer this awful fate at the hands of the alien government. Fortunately, the Roman soldiers routinely allowed this act of mercy for the doomed criminals.

Refused By The Suffering Servant

We have become accustomed to expecting the worst from people who have the opportunity to do in their enemies. However, it is not uncommon for those who have to carry out the job of being executioners to show some humaneness in their grizzly work. We can give credit to the unnamed Roman soldiers who were willing to offer this mixture of wine and gall as a sedative for Jesus. One can imagine that, as they regularly carried on this business of nailing people to crosses, they needed a sedative themselves. There is some evidence that the Roman soldiers made a drink themselves called *posca*, which was made of water, sour wine, and eggs. This work of crucifixion was an ugly business, and one can appreciate why the soldiers might be moved to offer a small token of kindness to Jesus. However, that is not the point of the evangelist in mentioning this matter.

What the evangelist underscores is that when Jesus tasted it, he would not drink it. Apparently, Jesus was willing to take something for the relief of his understandable thirst, but when he recognized the attempt to dull his senses, he refused. Jesus wanted to take the cup of suffering that the Father had handed to him. He had been prepared and strengthened for this hour in another way. In the Garden of Gethsemane he had already tasted of that cup and had determined that he would take it to its last draft. What was involved was not awful physical pain alone. As ugly and as dastardly as the crucifixion appeared to any who watched, the scene was all the more touching for those who deemed our Lord as innocent. For our Lord himself it was all the more weighty, because Jesus struggled with the full weight of knowing that all such scenes were necessary.

An Inadequate Drug

Jesus was more than an innocent victim of injustice. Jesus was contending with the false judgment of the world, its unbelief, and its lack of love. What Jesus had to bear as he suffered at the miserable hands of religious and civil courts would not have to take place for anyone if only humanity had not succumbed to its own self. What Jesus had proved, when he stood trial before the judges of religious and civil communities, was that even they were not capable of recognizing the best of God's revelation of grace and love.

As Jesus dealt with the reality of humanity's sin and the judgment of God upon that sin, Jesus was the catalyst for both. At this very moment God was exposing the futility and the inability of humanity to save itself. For that moment Jesus wanted to be fully conscious, fully aware, and fully cognizant that he might save the world from itself. With the full resources of all his senses, Jesus was offering himself to God in faith and to the world in love. The pain that surged through his extended body in throbbing smarts was matched with the pain that throbbed in his mind and tortured his heart. A drug that would have dulled his pain would not have been adequate for all that Jesus felt, but Jesus did not want it to interfere with what he wanted to feel for us.

We Did Our Best

Interestingly, the evangelist Mark records the harangue that was carried on by the criminals crucified with Jesus, the passersby, the chief priests, the elders, and the scribes in order to convince themselves that Jesus was not the Son of God or the promised King of Israel. All of these people taunted Jesus with the same temptation to prove himself to be the Son of God by coming down from the cross. On the tree of the cross Jesus was thrown back into Eden where the first temptation to Adam, the son of God, was to prove himself to be like the gods by eating of the tree of knowledge of good and evil. But the greatest temptation came in that moment when the fate of all of humankind hung in the balance as Jesus sensed that moment when he had to enter the final judgment of God, death. It was then, Mark says, after three hours of darkness, that Jesus realized the awful abandonment of God in death. "My God, my God, why have you forsaken me?" By faith, by trust, by surrender to God his Father, he would not be abandoned even in death. God was still his God. By faith he remained the Son of God. By faith he would not let go of God. By faith he would not be separated from God.

In that terrible moment as Jesus was suspended upon the cross, heaven and earth were drawn together in this tattered and bruised body and cemented together in that giant heart that pumped innocent blood through the veins of God's obedient Son. Mark notes that when some of the bystanders heard Jesus call out to God in the Hebrew, "Eli, Eli," they thought he was calling for Elijah. No doubt they figured that delirium had set in and the end was near. The Fourth Gospel also mentions that Jesus said, "I thirst." At that, one of the bystanders, according to Mark, not one of the soldiers, "ran and got a sponge, filled it with sour wine, put it on a stick, and gave it to him to drink." No doubt, when that person returned to the crowd, he or she said, "I did the best I could for him." We all like to be able to say that when we say our farewells to our friends or dear ones.

56

It Was Our Best

Whoever it was that offered the sour wine to our Lord undoubtedly did it out of sympathy and eagerness to do something for Jesus. Luther did not think much of that. He thought poorly of the idea of someone helping in this manner. For Luther it was an insult that someone would offer the Savior sour wine, or vinegar, in that moment when the Savior was exhausted from his ordeal of battling sin, death, and hell.

However, Luther probably gave no thought to the medicinal or sedative effects the sour wine was to offer. To be sure, the total effect had to be minimal in the face of what Jesus had endured. In that regard, it only serves to emphasize that there really is nothing that we can contribute to achieving our own salvation. Jesus had completed and finished what had to be done for the salvation of the world. He had refused sedation before entering that struggle with Satan, death, and hell. Now that it was over, he could be indulged. So the best that the lady or gentleman could offer was a few sips of sour wine.

It Was Accepted

Three of the evangelists agree that Jesus took this second attempt at sedation, though Mark indicates that the one who offered it called out that the people should wait to see if Elijah would come to take Jesus down from the cross. No one can tell if that was said in the form of a taunt or as a change of heart in one who had taunted him. What is important for us is to note that Jesus accepts this offer of sedation. As Jesus did, we think back to a parable he told about the rich man and Lazarus in Abraham's bosom. In hell and in torment the rich man asked Abraham to send Lazarus with a drop of water to come and cool his tongue. Now as Jesus has completed his suffering of our hell and death upon the cross he permits a sinner to come and to cool his tongue with sour wine.

We think also of how our Lord described his coming again to separate the sheep from the goats. When our Lord calls the sheep to inherit the kingdom with him, Jesus said they will be surprised to hear that our Lord took account of their service of love in giving

57

the thirsty something to drink and in visiting those who were in prison. So it was that, wittingly or unwittingly, a bystander served our Lord with a drink of sour wine when he was thirsty and visited him when our Lord was imprisoned by a cross as a criminal and insurrectionist. And our Lord accepted the drink.

Its Finality

As our Lord Jesus Christ accepted the gift of sour wine, he also gave indication that the battle was over. The struggle was finished. The work was done. Jesus in complete obedience to the Father had finished the long march from Bethlehem to Golgatha, from the manger to the cross. Passively Jesus had permitted the courts of the religious and civil communities to judge and condemn him. In so doing he had permitted God's judgment to fall hard on him that as one of us he could go to his death as a sinner.

Now it was over. A sip of sour wine from a sponge on a stick was a toast to heaven on our behalf. It is this same Christ who suffered, died, and rose again who comes to us as the living Christ under the form of wine in the Holy Eucharist that we might taste of the goodness of God. Probably most pastors sometime in their ministries hear the complaint from parishioners that the wine used in the celebration of Holy Communion was sour. So much the better. Let it be a reminder of how our Lord sipped from sour wine at that moment when he offered up complete and full our salvation to God. To be sure, when we taste of that sour wine, we should be drunk with the joy and gladness of knowing that our salvation is full and free.

The Spice
Of Death

Good Friday draws us to the cross of our Lord Jesus Christ that we might concentrate and meditate on our Lord's suffering. We dwell on each of those words that we hear from out of the darkness that we might wring the fullest meaning we can from that awe-filled scene where heaven and hell, judgment and salvation, God and man meet. What cannot be overlooked is the manner in which our Lord was buried. We do take note with considerable concern and care the manner in which friends and dear ones are buried. It is rather striking that, with the wave of criticism that was aimed at the practices of the undertaking profession a number of years ago, people continue to spend as much as they ever have for the burial of their dear ones. The reason, of course, is that people want to pay the highest respect they can for loved ones. Or sometimes it is guilt that prompts relatives to become lavish in doing the best they can for the deceased.

Whatever the motives of the living are for sending the dead to their graves in style, we do take note of the results. We draw our own conclusions about how the dead are buried. Most generally, our real estimate of what has been done for the deceased is how much love has been poured into the arrangements. The dollars do not make all the difference. It is the love that mounts up in what is accomplished. For that reason it is important for us to note that the evangelists took the pains to report our Lord's burial in some detail. We do have accounts of how members of the inner circle of Jesus' followers attended to the proper funeral rites for the corpse of our Lord. What they did is worth examination.

A Virtuous Act

To begin with, the two secret disciples of Jesus, Joseph of Arimathea and Nicodemus, were the ones who performed what was regarded as a virtuous act in the Hebrew community. The Hebrew people were very considerate about the burial of their dead. They did not go to the extent of the burial rituals their forebears may have witnessed in Egypt. The Hebrews did not embalm the dead in mummified form as did the Egyptians. Nor did the Hebrews place the dead body into a sarcophagus or coffin.

However, the Hebrews did bury their dead the same day of the person's death. Friends and family did process to the burial grounds. Attention was given to embalming the body with spices of various sorts. Respect was maintained for the burial ground. Not to have a decent burial was considered a disgrace. Special times were allotted for mourning. Periods of mourning for as long as thirty days were prescribed for notable figures. Mourning also took different forms. There was allowance for the emotional release at suffering loss. There were eulogies that bespoke only the good for the dead. There were also compositions of comfort and there were laments for great tragedies. In the case of our Lord's death, much of all this had to be omitted because of the lack of time.

A Confessional Act

While the burial of our Lord was all too brief and too private, we cannot emphasize enough how bold an act it was. The ones who took charge of the burial certainly knew that Hebrew tradition allowed that the worst of criminals and poorest of citizens should have a decent burial. However, they attended to Jesus at great risk. Joseph of Arimathea is described as "a disciple of Jesus, though a secret one because of his fear of the Jews." Nicodemus is remembered as the one "who at first had come to Jesus by night." Nicodemus is remembered elsewhere by the evangelist John as a leader of the Jews (3:1-15) and one who guardedly did ask for a fair trial of Jesus (7:50-52). However, Joseph now threw all caution to the winds and sought out the permission from Pilate to bury the body of Jesus.

People might explain that as a do-gooder condescending to do something on behalf of a down-and-outer to make himself feel good. However, Joseph was not handling this matter in a potter's field or something donated by the township trustee. Joseph took the body of Jesus to a garden and placed his body in a fresh tomb in which no one had been laid. That was a bold gesture that could cost Joseph the loss of a job and his prestige in the community. Likewise, Nicodemus may have been disgraced in the ruling order of the Pharisees and the Sanhedrin for participating in this right. That did not matter now. Joseph and Nicodemus did what the disciples did not hang around to do. The disciples had fled for their lives. Joseph and Nicodemus had remained that they might make their bold confession of faith and trust in the rabbi they now acknowledged as their teacher and master.

A Supreme Act

Not only did Joseph and Nicodemus act boldly, but they also acted out of the conviction that they were doing the last and the best that they could for the Lord Jesus. That may have been prompted somewhat by that guilt for not having done more before. However, most often when families do something for their dead loved one out of guilt, they can or do go on living their selfish ways as before the funeral.

For Joseph and Nicodemus life would never be the same now that they had boldly taken things into their hands. Not only were they renouncing their stations in life, but also they were taking new positions. At the moment they undoubtedly had no idea where this act would take them. Like the disciples and all other followers of Jesus, they did not anticipate the resurrection of our Lord at this time. That was not important at the moment. They knew they had to do these things for Jesus, who had taught them to live life differently than they had learned to live. They also knew that the life they had been living was the kind of lifestyle that led people to do the kind of thing they did to Jesus in the name of the law, righteousness, and God. They were acting with a newfound freedom that enabled them to do this good thing for Jesus. If this appeared to be the sign of a lost cause, it was the opposite for them. They had lost an old way of life and found a new freedom in Christ.

A Beautiful Act

One would also have to regard this act of Joseph and Nicodemus as a beautiful act. Nicodemus brought a "mixture of myrrh and aloes," according to John, "weighing about a hundred pounds," which would be about 75 pounds, according to our measurements. They then "took the body of Jesus and wrapped it with the spices in linen cloths, according to the burial custom of the Jews." One gets the impression that this was an act of beauty that went beyond normal requirements. Seventy-five pounds was a large amount to be used for this rite that was intended to soften the onset of the deterioration of the body. Little did Joseph and Nicodemus believe that the body of our Lord would not experience what we must all experience in death. What Joseph and Nicodemus did served to be purely aromatic and refreshing in the closed spaces of that new tomb. The new tomb would not have been contaminated with the stench of other decaying bodies. The new tomb must have been filled with the pleasant odors coming from the spices in which the ravaged and still body of our Lord was packed. This was not wasted on our Lord.

Matthew reported that when Jesus was still an infant wise men from the East came to worship the Holy Child with their gifts of gold, frankincense, and myrrh. We can well imagine that Mary and Joseph may have repeated the story for the boy as he was growing up as comfort and encouragement. Jesus had received a good many kudos during his life and ministry. However, the evangelists mention several times that he was anointed by women on his feet as expressions of their gratitude for forgiveness and as expressions of devotion. It is difficult to separate these several anointings with the possibility of one or two being versions of the same one. However, it is important to note that at Bethany when

Mary anointed Jesus, Judas protested the gesture as a waste of money. Jesus, however, replied, "Leave her alone. She bought it that she might keep it for the day of my burial." If in good grace Jesus accepted that gift as an act of love, angels must have been rejoicing as these two brave men anointed our Lord for his burial.

An Irrelevant Act

At the same time that we acknowledge how meaningful, how beautiful, and how confessional this act was from the Nicodemus and Joseph side of things, it was irrelevant to doing anything for Jesus or contributing to what had to be done to finish or complete his work. We should not be surprised. In that sense it is highly symbolic of the fact that there is nothing, absolutely nothing we can do for God. We cannot contribute anything to God's needs.

As helpless as the dead Christ was, Jesus had already accomplished what had to be done for the salvation of the world. The spices were not even necessary for a body that would not see decay. The linen shroud would not be able to contain a living and resurrected Christ. The spices would leave their aroma for all who would come to see. All that says to us that there is nothing we can do for our salvation either. No matter how beautiful the act, how large the contribution, how serious the motives, nothing adds to the eternal gift won and given to us by our Lord Jesus Christ.

An Act of Certainty

If the act of the burial of our Lord with the costly spices in a beautiful new tomb in Joseph's lovely garden was irrelevant as far as contributing to our salvation, it was nonetheless very important from another point of view. It was an act certainly. It was all legal. Joseph had obtained an official permit for the burial rite. Mark mentions that Pilate did not grant this permit until he had been assured by an officer that Jesus was truly dead. Once that permit was granted, Joseph and Nicodemus proceeded with funeral arrangements which they had to hurry, because the Jewish Sabbath began at six o'clock Friday evening. No work could be done from that hour until the Sabbath was finished at six o'clock the next evening. When Joseph and Nicodemus did complete their work of removing the body from the cross, transporting it to the empty tomb, and embalming it in the linen with the special spices, they could leave the tomb with the assurance that Jesus was dead. John did not mention it, but each of the other three evangelists reported that some women followed the procession to the tomb and saw where the body was laid.

There was no doubt about it. Jesus was dead and buried. There were sufficient witnesses to make the fact stand up in court. If later there would be those who would steal the body of Jesus and say something had happened to him to simply list him among the missing, they could testify otherwise. Jesus had been properly carried as a corpse and his body had been laid to rest. Jesus did die for sure. Strangely enough, later on, the enemies of our Lord were the ones to accuse the disciples of doing this very thing. However, as the enemies tried to create rumors to that effect, the evidence Joseph, Nicodemus, and the women could produce could drown out the unsubstantiated with the evidence we all now confess, "He suffered under Pontius Pilate, was crucified, died and was buried."

A Redeemed Act

The certainty of the burial of Jesus was also redeemed and made all the more sure and valuable by our Lord himself. On the morning of the third day it was Mary Magdalene, according to John, who went to the tomb first and found it empty. She ran to the disciples, Peter and John, to report that someone had stolen the body of Jesus. However, when the disciples ran to the tomb, they were stunned by what they found. To be sure, the tomb was empty as Mary had said. However, they found the linen wrappings lying there. The cloth that had been placed on Jesus's head was on a separate pile, rolled up by itself.

At that moment we are not sure what Peter and John thought. John wrote, "The other disciples ... saw and believed." But we do not know what he believed, because John adds, "For as yet they did not understand the scripture, that he must rise from the dead. Then the disciples returned to their homes." The evidence they found was that Jesus was gone, but his burial cloths were empty and neatly left behind. What they could not yet know nor imagine is even difficult for us to picture. Jesus rose from the dead that morning, as we know, to demonstrate the fullness of his victory over sin, death, and hell. We do not know how he appeared, but it is nice to imagine that he just might have taken the time not only to arrange neatly the burial cloths but also take time to smell the wonderful spices with which Joseph and Nicodemus had embalmed him.

Easter
Jogging

He is Risen. "He is Risen, indeed," we respond. We sound the trumpet. We decorate the altar in gold. We sound the bells. We sing out the alleluia's in the loudest crescendo we can. We turn out in larger numbers than any other time of the church year to celebrate this Queen of Feasts. And well we should. No matter how large the observance and how great the celebration we cannot make it grand enough to capture the fullness of its meaning for us. We are always going to have trouble with Easter because, no matter how hard we try, the full import and the full impact of what God does for us at Easter eludes us.

However, if we think we have trouble with Easter, think of the poor dear people in the city of Jerusalem that first Easter. The townspeople must have been troubled by the rumors that were flying around. We know that the enemies of Jesus were completely unnerved by the presence of the empty tomb. Yet the people who had the most trouble with Easter were none other than the disciples of our Lord. It is a most striking feature of all the Easter Gospels that not one of them portrays a hero who claims to know that this is what the disciples should have expected. Not one of them says, "We should have known this was going to happen." It did not dawn on a single member of our Lord's company to say, "After all of the surprises, the wonderful things that we have heard our Lord

67

say, and the miraculous things we have seen him do, we should have anticipated this greatest of all miracles."

It's A Race

If you and I were writing a script about the way Easter should have been, we probably would have made believers out of thousands of people that first Easter Day. At least we would have made believers out of the disciples. The evangelists are honest. They tell us how it really was. The disciples are stunned. They are surprised. They are filled with fear. We have no evidence that they believed. They were filled with emotion and acted with a great deal of commotion.

The Holy Gospel appointed for this Easter Day reports some of the confusion of that first Easter. There was much running. If you were one of the neighbors along the way taking your dog out on a morning stroll, imagine what would go through your mind as you witness the traffic going to and from that tomb! Mary is in a hurry to get there the first thing in the morning. It is still dark when she sets out to complete the embalmment procedures for Jesus. She sees the stone rolled away from the door, so she runs back to see the disciples. She tells Peter and John, who immediately run to the tomb. Old Peter, who probably could not have run across the street to catch a good sale, runs all the way. And young John gets there first.

More Running

Mary must have run back again, too, because when the disciples return to the others, also probably on the run, Mary remains in the garden. We can imagine that a neighbor on the road that morning would have suspected that something was up. Something important was happening. If we saw that much running today we might think that our neighbors were out holiday jogging. If something of this importance would happen in our neighborhood we would hear cars racing, tires screeching, and sirens screaming. All this running, however, was not out of joy and happiness. These disciples were running scared. They were filled with fear. The second Holy Gospel listed for this day is from Matthew, who mentions several times how fear seized the people. In this case, Mary was filled with fear, because she was sure that someone had taken the body of Jesus away.

What else could Mary think when she saw the stone had been rolled away? The stone had been put in place and the tomb had been sealed, because the enemies had thought that the disciples would come and steal the body and say that Jesus had risen from the dead. But now that the stone is rolled away, Mary does not even consider the possibility that Jesus would be risen from the dead. She is sure that the enemies have come and taken the body of Jesus away. That was a natural deduction. Charlie Chaplin was stolen from his grave. When that happened did anyone propose that he was risen from the dead? Did his family come forward to suggest that Charlie had talked about rising from the dead or about the notion that he was immortal? Even those who suggest that the character that Charlie played in the silent movies is immortal did not suggest that his tomb is empty because he is still alive.

Death Is Death

Death is death. None was prepared for the event of the resurrection of Jesus of Nazareth from the dead. He had been sealed in the tomb. The process of decomposing should have begun. The dehydration of cells, the return to dust, should have started. Mary makes the logical deduction that if Jesus had moved from the tomb someone had to carry him out feet first. The disciples who come to see the tomb make the same deduction. They do not yet believe that Jesus is risen, but they believe with Mary that he had been carried away.

When the disciples confirm Mary's fears, she remains there in tears. Later on when she suspects that it is a friendly person who speaks to her, it had to be the gardener who had moved Jesus for some reason. If it was not the enemy, it was some friend who had moved Jesus for a good reason. Death still controlled the thoughts of the disciples this first Easter morn. The empty tomb is not proof for them that Jesus is risen. So entrenched were they in their grief, so locked were they in the grip of their mourning, that they could not even guess that Jesus might possibly be risen from the dead.

69

There is not one shred of evidence that the disciples even remotely suspected that Jesus was risen from the dead.

Death Is The Spoiler

We do not find it difficult to understand why the disciples did not recognize the significance of the empty tomb. All of us are so oriented to the world of death we are all caught in its cold grip. Mary wanted to hold on to a corpse. The Hebrews considered it a great tragedy if a person's remains were disturbed in any way. To have the grave robbed was a dreadful violation of one's person who should rest in peace with one's fathers. Mary considered all that, to be sure. But she wanted to be able to attend to his corpse: to give it a good scent, to apply some cosmetics perhaps, to hide death, and to hold on to Jesus. She had all the same pain and hurt we have when we find it so difficult to say good-bye to our dear ones. We hold them even when rigor mortis has stiffened the bodies for days. We have a hard time pushing off from the caskets. Death is the spoiler for us.

Even on Easter itself, we are liable to say, "How much better it would be if our dear one were still here." We permit death to rule our emotions and our hearts and to deaden our sensitivity to the possibility that death may not be the final word. There is a reason for that. What lies beneath this easy capitulation to death is not simply our fear that death is so final, but our deeper fear that it is a judgment. No matter how brave we may be, or even if we entertain death wishes, or we are convinced that death is natural to the creation, we have to face the fact that death cuts us off from everything. All of the fears that haunt us are related to the specter that death is judgment.

According To The Word

No wonder then that our Easter evangelists spend so much time explaining to us how frightened and how confused the disciples were. Mary's word is right. "They have taken him away." The disciples believed her. Then John adds, "For as yet they did not understand the scripture, that he must rise from the dead." They believed he was stolen from the empty tomb, because they did not believe the Word. And Matthew tells us in his Gospel that the Easter angel told the women, "He is not here; for He has risen as He said." Jesus had given them the Word. They did not believe the Word. That is why there was all this confusion, this disbelief, the unbelief, the fear that Easter morning. They could have believed the Word, and they would have known. They could have believed the Word and they would have been spared all this grief and heartache. They could have believed the Word, and they would have known exactly what to do Easter morning. The scriptures had said it. Jesus had said it, and everything that he did and all that he had taught pointed in this direction. But they did not believe because they themselves were still the children of death and they had to live out their fears. Had they been children of the Word, they would have been able to set their own watch at the tomb to await his Easter appearance.

The Witness

However, we cannot fault the disciples too much because we would have acted exactly the same way and still do. That is why the evangelists are so honest about their own confusions that day. They tell us how they identify with our fears and doubts. Now, however, they have left us abundant witness to the fact that Jesus is indeed risen from the dead and that we have no reason to fear. Looking back on it, John says the disciples should have known from the Word. Matthew says they should have remembered that he said he would rise again. John says when they looked into the tomb they should have seen the witness. "He saw the linen wrapping lying there, and the cloth that had been on Jesus' head, not lying with the linen wrappings but rolled up in a place by itself."

People who would rob a grave would not take the time to do all this neat folding of the napkin on his head. They might have dropped it in their haste to get out of there. Nor would they leave the linen cloths. They would have simply run out with him. So John gives the evidence that the rumor about stealing the body of Christ just does not make sense in face of the facts. The empty tomb together with the neatly arranged burial linens with the Word are the evidences that Jesus is truly risen. It is through the Word

71

that the Risen Christ still comes to us. He is that lively Word by which He still comes to give us life and hope. In the sacrament today Jesus comes as the victorious and living Christ who says, "Here I am living that in me you might have life and hope. Here I am living that in me you might have the resurrection hope. Here I am that in me you have the seeds of eternal life."

What all this means for us is that we are now able to live in a world in which we see signs of life, and we are able to live as those oriented to heaven and not to the signs of death. All of life as the world lives it is shaped by death. We can live in contradiction of the signs of the tomb and death. We are able to bring the message of today's Epistle to anyone who lies at death's door. "You have been raised with Christ, seek the things that are above." The families caught up in the grief of mourning the death of family members know their loved ones live with the Risen Christ. We can get on the phone to offer condolences to neighbors who suffer the sudden losses in the light of the resurrection. We can be cheered by confident joy that enables an Easter celebration. It is the power and joy of Easter that we do not simply live in the hope of the resurrection but that the resurrection itself is the source of how we live in defiance of the world of death and sin. Jesus lives. Because he lives, we too shall live.

Easter
Power

Storms that knock out electrical systems make us mindful of how dependent we are upon power. High winds deprive us of power. When we do not lose power in devastating storms we are most grateful, realizing how dependent we have become on the utility companies. However, it is significant that the primary definitions of power do not relate to the matter of energy or force. The first definitions of power have to do with the possession of control, authority, or influence over others. There is a whole battery of synonyms for power that describe power as the ability to direct or restrain others. We, of course, confront that kind of power daily in our vocations in working with others, in our homes, regulating the lives of our family, in all organization of life all the way to the ruling of nations.

We also know how some people have the natural gifts for applying power. Some are born to power. Others seek power. Some abuse power. The whole matter of authority, jurisdiction, control, command, or dominion is an extremely intriguing one. Often we are locked in international and national debates as to how we should or should not use power. The Holy Gospel appointed for today announces how our Lord Jesus Christ conferred enormous powers upon his followers when he appeared to them as the Risen Christ. That story places at your disposal the same kind of Easter power.

The Evidence

The Fourth Gospel account of our Lord's resurrection appearance takes place on Easter in the Upper Room where the disciples had gathered. The appearance appears to be substantiated by the other Gospel account in Luke. The disciples were quite obviously in a state of shock. They were completely drenched with fear because of what might happen to them in the light of the disappearance of Jesus from the tomb. They are locked in the Upper Room as a defense against anyone who might be seeking them out. However, it is Jesus who looks them up.

According to the Johannine account Jesus comes and stands among them unannounced. This is a strange new way for him to come to his disciples. He is not confined to the normal and natural ways for a human to come into the room. Yet the Risen Christ is able to communicate with the disciples. The very first thing that he does is to give them the evidence of what had taken place. He reintroduces himself as their Lord and Master. His credential for claiming his place in the center of their lives is a scar. He is able to show them the badges of honor he wore because of his crucifixion. He has five scars. They are the nail prints in hands and his feet and the wound where he was lanced in the side as proof of his death. John says that what he showed that evening were his hands and his side, the living proof that it was he, Jesus of Nazareth, who was among them. The scars were also the visible signs that he had been dead, and that it was he who was now alive among them.

Shalom

When Jesus appeared to the disciples, his greeting was, "Peace be unto you." The Hebrew word *shalom,* for "peace," is a most comprehensive word, covering the full realm of relationships in daily life and expressing an ideal state of life. The word suggests the fullness of well-being and harmony untouched by ill fortune. The word as a blessing is a prayer for the best that God can give to enable a person to complete one's life with happiness and a natural death. If the concept of *shalom* became all too casual and light-hearted with no more significance than a passing greeting, Jesus came to give it new meaning. At Bethlehem God announced that peace would come through the gift of God's unique Son. The mission and ministry of our Lord made it quite clear that Jesus had come to introduce the rule of God and to order peace for the world. However, this rule stood in stark contrast to the warring factions of the world which seek to find their own peace in other ways.

Jesus came to witness to his unbroken relationship with his Father as the chief sign of peace. In a world of adversity and strife this was his gift to his disciples and was to contradict any other form of security offered by the world. Jesus also taught that this gift of peace was dependent upon his complete victory over sin and death. It should not have been unexpected then that our Lord would greet the disciples warmly with "Peace," and display for them the scars which are the signs of his victory over the arch enemies of sin and death. So it was that the community of the faithful came to look upon the life, death, and resurrection of our Lord Jesus Christ as God's Gospel of Peace for the whole world. Apostolic greetings also were to announce the peace that finds its power, meaning, and significance in the life, death, and resurrection of our Lord.

A Breath Of Life

In addition to this most welcome greeting for his disciples, our Lord "breathed on them and said to them, 'Receive the Holy Spirit.'" That scene reminds us of another in the Garden of Eden. "Then the Lord God formed man from the dust of the ground, and breathed into his nostrils the breath of life; and the man became a living being" (Genesis 2:7). On that Easter evening our Lord made new creatures of his disciples. Paul wrote later, "If anyone is in Christ, there is a new creation: everything old has passed away; see, everything has become new!" (2 Corinthians 5:17).

The One who comes from the grave brings with him the new life, the life that has conquered death and reconciled us to God. As the One victorious over death breathes, he breathes into his disciples the new life in which reconciliation with God is the new and perfect relationship that makes people blameless in the court of the living God and enables them to do God's will among people. This new life, which is conferred by the power and force of the

75

Holy Spirit, is synonymous with eternal life. The Holy Spirit enables those who share in the victory of our Lord to opt for decisions that make for peace and are conducive to actions of freedom and love. It's a new way of living.

The Absolution

The victory our Lord achieved by dying to destroy death for us was a significant victory. This was no hollow victory. We think of the problems we have in trying to determine what we have achieved in our swift and brilliant victories in previous wars. Sometimes our victories haunt us. Sometimes they are ambiguous. Too often the victories are only momentary. Not so with our Lord's decisive victory over the grave. Jesus comes from the grave with an authority he could now share in a meaningful way with his disciples. What God achieved through the death and resurrection of his Son could now be put into universal practice. God had reconciled the world unto himself. God said there was now a basis for God and people to live together. That was our Lord Jesus Christ himself. His death and resurrection became the action or act by which God reconciled the world to himself.

Consequently, Jesus could give the authority from heaven to his disciples, "If you forgive the sins of any they are forgiven; if you retain the sins of any, they are retained." That is divine authority. That is authority more powerful than any human authority. With that authority you can make lives new. By that authority you reconcile people to yourself. By that authority you can reconcile people one to another. By the same authority you can withhold the forgiveness in the hope that the objects of your love will awaken to their need to seek out the goodness and mercy of God. You can withhold the forgiveness of God from those who neither love nor trust the God who created them.

The Effect

The effect of the power that Jesus brought from the grave is far reaching. It is the real power the world needs for being healed. The brokenness of the world is its inability to live in harmony in marriage, family, work, community, political, national, and international relationships. That should be obvious and apparent to everyone. We all suffer from the problem at one level or another, and generally from more than one level at a time. However, what is not so obvious is that people are inept at overcoming the destructiveness of bad human relations. The nursery rhyme is correct about Humpty Dumpty, who had the great fall. "All the king's horses and all the king's men couldn't put Humpty together again." But God can and does through the power of the forgiveness he shares with us.

Husband and wife can forgive each other to make their marriage new every day. Parents and children can forgive all the failures they have in their daily efforts to live together in tranquility. Relationships at work will fare far better with those who are forgiving people than they will with those who hew legalistically to the personnel manuals. In the community, progress will be and can be made when there are significant persons who are able to be advocates and reconcilers in the human relations that always suffer from the push people make for their individual rights and for their special agendas. The people who have the real power at the top in international situations are those who can practice the art of reconciliation. One editorial stated that one of the problems we had in the Middle East was that our Secretary of State came at his task out of Christian traditions, and it is difficult to work with those peoples who do not have the same convictions. Yet how important it was that he tried.

Faith

As the Risen Christ bestowed the gift of the Holy Spirit upon the twelve, he also empowered them to believe. John's account of this meeting in the Upper Room is the Johannine version of what happened at Pentecost. The disciples received the gift of the Holy Spirit that they might believe and understand how it was that Jesus was the Messiah. Their fear turns to joy and they are able to witness to the Christ. When Thomas returns to the Upper Room after his absence for the meeting with Jesus, the disciples are able to report, "We have seen the Lord."

77

Thomas cannot believe the account the disciples gave him. He says that he can believe only if he sees the scars of our Lord's death. It is interesting that he demands the signs of death rather than of life. However, Jesus does return a week later when Thomas is present. Jesus offers to let Thomas touch the scars as Thomas had requested. Thomas is able to forego that request and confesses his faith. Jesus then says to him, "Have you believed because you have seen me? Blessed are those who have not seen and yet have come to believe." Jesus certainly did not intend to put down Thomas or his faith. What was important, however, was to make it clear that faith is a miracle. It is the Holy Spirit who has the power to create faith in the hearts of people. The Holy Spirit works that miracle in helping people to believe in the Christ who has achieved our salvation for us.

Believe!

John concludes his Gospel with the words, "Now Jesus did many other signs in the presence of his disciples, which are not written in this book. But these are written so that you may come to believe that Jesus is the Messiah, the Son of God, and that through believing you may have life in his name." The phenomenon of the Christ Event, the Easter Christ, the Risen Christ, is that power is now available to us that enables us to be assured that as certainly as Jesus rose from the death of the crucifixion for sins, we, too, shall rise again. In the meantime we have been placed on special status. Jesus said to the disciples, "As the Father has sent me, so I send you." As God's reconciliation of the world was achieved through our Lord Jesus Christ, so now God sends us into the world as the practitioners of this reconciliation.

Begin where we will, we will have no end of opportunities to share with people the need they have for the forgiveness of sins. Our own lives beg for forgiveness. Wherever there are people, there is need for the forgiveness of sins. And it is within our power. One does not have to be a bishop or a pastor. Every Christian has the power to forgive, and when he or she does, "it is as valued and certain in heaven also as if Christ, our dear Lord, dealt with us himself." The baton has been passed on. Jesus confessed that the work he did was given him by the Father. Now he passed on the gift and powers to the Holy Spirit, who serves as his clone in the role of counselor. And now it has been passed on to us.

Easter
Understanding

Edward Schillebeeckx, an outstanding Roman Catholic New Testament Scholar, some twenty years ago published in Holland his work titled *The Understanding of Faith*. Schillebeeckx made a most incisive effort to explain how Christians can understand their faith in the modern world. In doing so, he also had to carefully delineate the function of language in general. There are definite rules for the use of language. There are rules for the interpretation of language. Not only must Christians ask how the interpretation of their faith stands up in the light of modern thought and analysis, but they must also make their interpretation of the faith stand up among Christians. It is not difficult to point out that there are breakdowns in communication with the world as to significance of the Christian Gospel. However, it is also true that the communications between Christians are also not the best.

In spite of the fact that one denomination after another claims total allegiance to the scriptures, we have significant differences in interpretation. Then there are the so-called non-denominational Bible study groups who come along to tell us they will clear up the communications by taking everything literally, and all they do is muddy the waters. What Schillebeeckx set out to do was to find a common way in which we understand how we can go about the task of interpretation that will cut through the complex issues that make understanding difficult. In the Holy Gospel for today we hear how our Lord Jesus Christ himself had to deal with these issues with his own disciples.

The Bible Is Not Enough

You recognize the setting for the Holy Gospel for today as being the Upper Room, the night of the first Easter day. This is the Evangelist Luke's account of what we heard from the Fourth Gospel last Sunday. Luke records in the same manner how Jesus suddenly appeared to his disciples and greeted them. While both evangelists mention that Jesus displayed his scars, Luke mentions just how frightened the disciples were. Luke describes the confused emotions of the disciples most aptly. He says, "In their joy they were disbelieving and still wondering."

After Jesus convincingly ate of a broiled fish in their presence, Jesus deliberately talked to them about what had happened. He explained that this is what he had been telling them all along while he was with them. He had spoken to them on the basis of what had been in the scriptures. He had talked to them on the basis of Moses, the prophets and the psalms. Still they had not understood when he had been teaching and preaching to them. Now they had not understood what he had accomplished by coming to them in the Risen Christ. They did not believe with Jesus sitting right at their dinner table. To have the Bible, the scriptures, obviously was not enough. All those Bible classes they had attended with him did not clarify the issues. They did not understand. The communication of the Bible as such did not stand up for them.

Words About God Are Not Enough

We should also recognize that words about God were not enough for the disciples. It is very safe to say that the disciples must have had endless talks, debates, and dialogues among themselves about what Jesus meant to them. This we can safely surmise from the kind of discussions Jesus had with them. Over and over again we know that his teaching was designed to point them to the future. He was very careful to try to prepare them for the time when he would no longer be with them as just one of them. In this past Lenten season we reviewed how Jesus tried to create in them an awareness of what he had to confront in his death and resurrection. Listening to all that Jesus taught and preached, as well as what he did, had to provoke considerable speculation among the disciples. In addition the disciples had to be impacted by all the public debate about Jesus. They had to hear from friends, neighbors, and strangers about their involvement with this public figure.

There was talk, talk, talk, and more talk about Jesus. No wonder then that at one point Jesus asked the disciples what the people were saying about him. The disciples had all kinds of answers. When Jesus asked them who they thought he was, Peter could give the quick reply that they believed Jesus was the Messiah (Mark 8:27-30). However, when Jesus was crucified they did not understand. Also, when Jesus came to them as the Risen Savior, they did not understand. All their speculation, all their talking, all their consorting with one another and with others did not help them face this moment when they had to ask who Jesus really was. Thus, the Bible and human reason were insufficient in helping them to understand Jesus and his finest hour.

Literalism Is Not Enough

Well, the literalists and the historians would jump in at this point and say that what it takes is proof. If you can come up with the evidence and you can prove how something happened, then people will have to believe. That will not be enough either. There the disciples were in the Upper Room with the Risen Christ, and they could not believe their own eyes. The problem was they could not understand with their hearts. Jesus had to address that. He volunteered to let them handle him. He had to correct their notions that he may have been some kind of apparition like a ghost. He could tell that even that was not convincing. He ate a fish which he requested of them. Luke makes the point that he did it in their presence.

Jesus did everything to fill the need for people to satisfy their senses and perceptions of what had transpired. Yet that was not enough. They sat there stupefied. People live with the signs of

God's providence, goodness, and mercy every day and still they do not believe what they should about God. People believe about the Bible and believe all kinds of things about God, but they do not believe with understanding. No matter how close they come to the kingdom, they are not true believers if they cannot recognize this crucified and Risen Christ who comes to them. That was the plight of the disciples. "In their joy they were disbelieving and still wondering." However, Jesus made believers out of them.

The Continuity

Jesus made believers out of the disciples by rehearsing for them the continuity of what God had been doing and saying all along. As the Risen Christ, Jesus sat there once again as the teacher of the disciples. He had to inform them that what he was telling them now was not different from what he had been saying to them all along. He said, "These are my words that I spoke to you while I was still with you — that everything written about me in the law of Moses, the prophets and the Psalms must be fulfilled." What Jesus meant was not simply that the Hebrew Scriptures were filled with predictions about the fact that Jesus would come. That would be a very thin and shallow interpretation of the value of the Hebrew tradition and witness. Rather, our Lord himself is present in the whole revelation of what God did and was doing for God's people.

The sense in which Jesus fulfilled the witness of the Hebrew Scriptures was not that Jesus simply did something that someone had foreseen he would do. Instead, Jesus fulfilled the scriptures in the sense that everything that God had done for the world and God's people through the centuries, God had now done in the life of our Lord Jesus Christ. What God did in the life, mission, and ministry of our Lord Jesus Christ gave meaning to everything he had revealed previously. The world did not have to wait for Jesus in order to be sure that God was in the world. God had been in the world and moving everything around the whole time. In Jesus, God gave us a close-up of what he had been doing. In Jesus, God also summarized what we can expect of God in the best and worst situations.

The Suffering As Key

As Jesus shared "everything written about him" with the disciples, "he opened their minds to understand the scriptures." The key to the scriptures was not what Mary Baker Eddy taught. It was the opposite of what she said. It was the opposite of what all those preachers of health and wealth teach. Jesus said to the disciples, "Thus it is written, that the Messiah is to suffer and to rise from the dead on the third day." The controlling element of the interpretation and understanding of the scriptures is that God is present in the death and resurrection of our Lord Jesus Christ. Now you cannot understand that apart from the Hebrew Scriptures, and you cannot understand the Hebrew Scriptures apart from what Jesus was saying.

Jesus sat there as the proof positive of how it all hung together. Jesus died in the world of sin and death to atone for the sins of the world and to destroy death by his perfect death. It was a perfect death not because he died beautifully. His death could not have been uglier. He died as a victim of injustice and the wrath of God. He died of crucifixion, regarded by Romans as the absolute worst of death sentences. Yet his death was perfect because he died trusting his Father, who had commissioned him to suffer what he must for the trespasses of the sinful and unbelieving world. It was a perfect death, because Christ did not surrender to death, but in perfect trust offered himself to his Father when death came. And God raised him on the third day.

For Forgiveness

Jesus did not leave it at that. He said, "The Messiah is to suffer and to rise from the dead on the third day, and that repentance and forgiveness of sins is to be proclaimed in his name to all nations." That is the purpose of all the activity of God and the purpose of the life, death and resurrection of our Lord Jesus Christ. People are to be made believers so that they know they can repent of their sins before God and be forgiven by this gracious and Holy God who delights in sharing his righteousness with us. A literal and yet more free translation of this would be, "Repentance for the forgiveness of sins should be proclaimed as Gospel." We have to get it straight. It is not enough to believe that there is a God. Not enough to believe something about God. Not enough to believe that God is all powerful or that God can punish.

When the Hebrews lingered as slaves in Egypt, even Pharaoh could say a number of times that he believed something about God. Pharaoh could also admit that he had sinned. Yet Moses knew Pharaoh did not trust and love God. Nor should we think it is remarkable if people say that they believe there is a god. To believe God is to be able to trust that our God forgives us in the Lord Jesus Christ. The point is that God has reconciled us to himself through his Son, our Lord, that God forgives us and that he will also raise us from the dead. That is why we can understand the Scriptures. We can understand them if we begin with that faith and trust in God, who is the Lord of life and death.

You Are Witnesses

Jesus knew that the disciples did not catch on fully as yet. He said that the movement to get this word out about the gracious God would have to begin at Jerusalem. There, he said, "You are witnesses of these things. And see, I am sending upon you what my Father promises; so stay here in the city until you have been clothed with power from on high." That was setting the stage for Pentecost when the disciples did get the message loud and clear and were able to preach with power the Gospel of our Lord Jesus Christ. It all began with faith and trust in God.

The disciples grew in their understanding of the scriptures because they had this saving faith to begin with. At the same time for fifty days they kept reading the scriptures with the understanding Jesus gave them, and the scriptures enlarged their faith to propel them into their great movement of witnessing and missionizing. That was the conclusion made by the Roman Catholic scholar Schillebeeckx. After a thoughtful and studied examination of the rule for communication, the whole business of language and its implications, he stated it quite aptly. He wrote that theology, that is a system of study about the word of God, is nonsense without faith. At the same time, faith without a theology is "hardly worthy of the name of faith." What we should come away with from the

86

Upper Room today is that our Lord taught us that the key to understanding the scriptures is his death and resurrection, which should be for the preaching of the forgiveness of sins, and that we can enhance that faith by continuing to read what the whole scriptures say about him.

He
Shepherds Us!

Andrew Young, former delegate to the United Nations and former mayor of Atlanta, finally published the book he claims he should have written ten years ago. The book, *The Way Out of No Way*, contains Young's observations about how real change occurs. He notes that changes for the better do not happen simply because we teach people how to work better or harder. Reforms take place when people exert their spirituality to achieve change. In his aristocratic and very intelligent manner, Mr. Young uses both personal and public experiences to make his points. Most certainly, the most obvious to all of us has been the civil rights movement which was inspired and achieved by both white and black churches. It was in that experience that many people learned that the only kind of life worth living is one that one is willing to die for. However, such an achievement also helps us to question seriously our concepts of power for effecting change.

We may imagine that we give or confer power equally. However, the one who moves into the seat of power may understand how that power is to be used in a completely different way from the predecessors in the same office. The marks of power are different for the variety of people on whom the power is conferred. Most generally, the people in power do not reveal openly their strategies for dealing with power. They just act. In direct contrast to that, in the Holy Gospel for today, we hear how our Lord Jesus perceived his role as our Leader, our Good Shepherd, and how he also understood the nature of the power which was given to him by his Father.

An Understanding Shepherd

The first thing that our Lord reveals about his understanding of his role and his authority is that he is highly sensitive to our problems. He indicates that other shepherds are hirelings who think first of self-preservation. They want to save themselves first. They see the wolf coming and run in the other direction. Jesus intimates that he sees the wolves coming also. He is conscious of what attacks are made on our lives. He is aware of the problems that we have to face. He knows what we must endure. He is alert to the many difficulties that we must face. That is important for us to understand.

What Jesus makes clear about his claim to power is that he so completely identifies with our problems that he is perfectly willing to lay down his life for us. What makes Jesus so sensitive to what we must endure is that he had the same enemies and the same problems confronting him. It was not as though Jesus was merely trying to understand what we have to face. He faced all the same difficulties. He was acutely aware of how intense our enemies are. For him they were always first and new temptations. They did not come from within his own being as so many do for us. We need to know that, and we should be especially comforted by that when we feel we are all alone in our temptation.

An Intimate Shepherd

Not only does our Good Shepherd know about our problems, but he also knows us. This knowing is not just acquaintanceship. This is not a casual relationship. He does not just happen to know us by sight. When our Good Shepherd talks about knowing us, he is talking about a unique intimate relationship. Some of us can remember that when we were children our mother or father could figure out what we were doing. It was a puzzle to us when Mom or Dad could anticipate what kind of trouble we were going to get into. It was equally a surprise when they could tell us when we had done something wrong even though they were not there. My mother left me with the distinct impression that she had eyes in the back of her head. She was also expert at reading the body language: a blush, the nervous twitch, the quiet movement. All were dead giveaways by which Mother knew me. And she knew me "inside and out" as she liked to say. It's that intimate kind of "knowing" that our Good Shepherd speaks of.

Jesus says he knows his own. He knows them as his very own. He has lived and died to make them his own. Consequently, his own know him. We know what Jesus the Christ is like, because he did live and die for us. It is by his great sacrificial act that we know what he is like. We know the full extent of his love. There may be some things we do not know about him, but we know what he is like and what a price he had to pay for making us his own. That helps us to read him like a book. He literally lived out the Word for us by suffering and dying. Because we know this about him, we also know the Father. We know him as he knows the Father and the Father knows him. Because we know the Good Shepherd, we know that God is love.

The Loving Shepherd

What makes us absolutely certain of this love which the Father has for us and which we have come to know in his Son is that it is universal. When we feel depressed and blue, when we feel down and out, when we wonder who we are, we feel all alone and we are certain that no one has the same problem as we. Then if it dawns on us that other people do have the same problem, we may find some solace in that. The old saw is "Misery loves company." In reality, however, that is of little help. We may even see that other people have bigger problems than we. When that dawns on us, we may feel a little better, but not necessarily.

What is a source of great comfort and hope for us is that the Lord Jesus says that he loves all within the fold and that he loves others who are not of the fold. This is to say that his love is universal. Because it is universal, there can be absolutely no doubt that he loves us. As his sacrifice was for all, his love is for all. We

91

would always have to worry if God's love was selective. Then we would have to worry if we were included. But because God loves one and all by what he does for us through the Good Shepherd, we know for sure "He loves me!"

The Leading Shepherd

Many new denominational books of worship have rituals for the affirmation of baptism. There are a variety of ways we can affirm our baptism. Confirmation is the confirmands' affirmation of their baptism. However, we can affirm our baptism as we transfer from congregation to congregation or at times when others affirm the baptisms publicly. However, we actually affirm our baptisms when we confess our sins and are absolved or any other way we renew our faith in Christ. What we affirm is not something that we do or that we have done. We affirm that we believe what God has done for us in the Lord Jesus Christ through Holy Baptism. He has done it all to make us his own. That is what this beautiful text from Saint John says to us today. Our Good Shepherd leads us. What he emphasizes in such a rich way is his intimate relationship with us.

Most of us cannot appreciate fully the picture he draws for us here, because we may not be acquainted with shepherding. What we see in our western plains today is also different from what Jesus pictures for us. On our western prairies the shepherds drive huge flocks of sheep with their dogs and from their horses. What Jesus pictures is the more intimate scene of the town shepherd in modest rural areas who may gather the flock in the morning from the homes of townspeople and drive them out into the meadows. Or we see the shepherd who lives with the sheep out in the plain and drives them into the sheepfold at night and lies down at the entrance of the sheepfold to serve as the very door for the sheepfold itself.

All of us have some impression of the Good Shepherd imprinted on our hearts and minds. Commonly, officials have completely different views of the offices to which they are elected. The variety is a result most often from the different perceptions the officials have of themselves. People also have had and have confessed different conceptions and pictures of our Lord Jesus Christ. Some see him at one end as soft as a marshmallow and others at the other extreme picture him as a harsh judge. The variety of Christologies in between is very large.

However, our Lord gives the picture of himself to us. He is no softie, this Lord of ours. He is a heavyweight who drives our foes away from us. At the same time for us he is tender-hearted and full of compassion, love, and grace. He wants us to know how deep his attachment is for us. He says that he has plenty to back up what love he holds for us. He was able to lay down his life for us and take it up again. That is power to be sure. It was also the greatest love ever demonstrated in the world. It is out of that love that he shepherds us. Artists have attempted to paint this for us. Most of them have painted a beautiful, pastoral scene for us. What we need is the picture of the rugged Shepherd who is bloodied in his battle for us, but who also shows the serenity of his confidence and the warmth of his love. That is the Good Shepherd.

He Abides
In Us

John Updike once more revealed his remarkably brilliant powers of description in the novel *Brazil*. Updike shares his uncanny ability to portray the setting and landscape that surround his characters in order to highlight their nature and their roles. However, Updike's greatest gift is the manner in which he is able to crawl inside the characters to reveal their restless and frantic struggles to discover themselves. The principal characters in *Brazil* are Tristao and Isabel. Their love for each other survives a tormented parade of trials forced on them by family, nature, society, and the economy. Yet the end for them is as tragic as for Tristan and Isolde, whose names and whose roles are so similar. Purposefully, the reader is left to wonder a great deal about the significance of such relationships and, above all, the meaning of such lives.

Today the Holy Gospel suggests to us that life lived apart from our Lord Jesus Christ is meaningless and without purpose. Jesus himself talks about the need to be attached to him. We can readily appreciate the importance of relationship in a day when human relations are extremely difficult. What Jesus suggests, however, is that all human relations are dependent upon him.

The Cutoffs

It is not difficult to document how difficult human relations are today. The homeless, unattached, and lonely people of the world are in the news everyday. Whenever the latest statistics are revealed about the high incidence of divorce or the number of people living alone, most of us probably think to ourselves, "We knew it was bad, but we did not know it was that bad." Yet the epidemic of divorces and the large number of people living alone are only symptomatic of the breakdown of human relations in so many areas of life.

People feel cut off. They live lonely lives surrounded by people. It is true that people very often are cut off from their hometowns and their families geographically. In addition, the opportunities to create relationships are not all that easy in a highly technocratic society. We have become more dependent upon things than we are dependent upon people. Even the crude attempts we make at developing occasions for making relationships are all too superficial. Artificial attempts soon fail for their inability to create lasting relationships of commitment and lasting value. It is no wonder then that all of the popular talk shows put on exhibition the most bizarre cases of failed human relationships. We have learned not to be shocked at how utterly human relations can not only fail but also mess up people's lives. Oprah Winfrey and company daily parade for us how bankrupt humanity is of good wholesome relationships.

The Vinedresser

What Jesus says in the Holy Gospel about vines and the failure of vines offers insight into the poor human relations of our time. Yet what Jesus has to say has deeper significance. Obviously, we are to understand our dependence upon him for life, for the sustenance and for the redemption of life. Our total life is dependent upon him in every way. However, the point of this saying of Jesus is that the vine exists under the care and scrutiny of the Vinedresser. The Vinedresser, Jesus explains, is the Father. The Vinedresser has planted the vine for a purpose, and he expects the vine to produce fruit. The Vinedresser will do the nurturing of the vine to make fruit possible, but when the vine fails after all that he has done for it, it must be removed to wither on some trash pile.

Our Creator God has the right to make a judgment on our lives. God expects us to produce. God looks for us to give evidence of what God has invested in us. Our lives are under constant judgment. There is no way we can escape the responsibility for which we have been created. In the very same way we look for foliage on the vine, God scrutinizes our lives for some signs of productivity. All of creation exists under that searching examination by God. That searching comes into our lives in a variety of ways. God works through many means. God gets at us through nature, parents, superiors, government and what have you.

God's Standard

What we should appreciate about God's judgment is that it is more than likely quite different from what most of us expect. We have our own standards of judgment. They are not necessarily like God's. For example, we may know of two quadriplegics. One remains completely helpless, sits in the chair, or lies in bed. The other is a talented and gifted painter, who does beautiful landscapes by taking the paint brush into the mouth to achieve his work. We may compare only the two, and we miss the fact that the painter also puts to shame a whole bevy of people who produce nothing worthwhile even though they have use of all of their faculties.

It is not difficult for us to erect or choose standards that are really means for us to be able to rationalize some support for our own viewpoints. More often than not, we elect standards for satisfying our own egos. It is not difficult at all to create a whole range of contrasts in individuals. Yet we would not be able to judge them adequately, because we have no proper basis for judgment. However, that should give us the hint that the fruit which God looks for on the vine may be a surprise. God expects to see something on the vine that reflects what God has been doing for us. The fruit that God is looking for is the direct result of what God has been doing for us right along.

The Pruning

What Jesus is talking about as fruit is faith. We can be certain he is talking about faith, because he himself gives the clue. He says that those who are not bringing forth fruit will have to be pruned and thrown away. This is because they obviously are not drawing their life from Christ who is the Vine. They are cut off from Christ. Consequently, they are cut off from life. Their lives are fruitless and dead. They must be pruned and taken away and ultimately thrown into the fire. On the other hand, Jesus says to his disciples, "You have already been cleansed by the word that I have spoken to you." This is to say that Jesus has already cleansed, pruned, and trimmed his disciples that they might be able to yield the proper fruit. They did not cleanse themselves. They did not make themselves fit branches for bearing fruit. Jesus himself furnished them with the righteousness to make their fruit acceptable to the Divine Vinedresser.

The substance of the Fourth Gospel intimates that cleansing comes through the washing of Holy Baptism. For John, the expression "the word" is none other than our Lord Jesus Christ himself. The word which Jesus had shared with the disciples was what he had taught them, to be sure. Yet it was much more. Jesus had shared with the disciples the revelation of himself as the very Word of God. The disciples were given the life of the Vine through the sacrament and through the word. They were sustained by the Vine who is the Word. It is in furnishing life to his disciples that our Lord also furnishes righteousness to all their works. Our Lord not only redeems us but also redeems our works that when the Vinedresser comes to judge us or look for fruit, God does not find us wanting.

The Good Fruit

The Holy Gospel appointed for today was a favorite text of Martin Luther. Luther lectured on and on to illuminate this passage. For him this was one more convincing piece of the scriptures that helps us to understand that we are saved by faith and not by our works. Without Christ, the true Vine, who himself suffered painful pruning at the hands of God through suffering, crucifixion, and death, no one can produce anything acceptable to God. Yet when we are cleansed by our Lord through baptism and the word we do produce works imbued with the righteousness that flows to us through the Vine.

In like manner Jesus taught that a bad tree cannot bring forth good fruit. First, the bad tree must be made whole through proper pruning and fertilizing. Luther was very explicit in describing the pruning and fertilizing in barnyard terms. Yet he rhapsodized on the encouragement and comfort this passage has for every Christian. When the Vinedresser comes looking for fruit, those branches which are in Christ offer the evidence that their lives are in Christ, because their works are furnished with his righteousness. Christians do not have to worry whether they are acceptable to God. Christ has made them and their works acceptable.

More Produce

There is another comforting feature of this saying of Jesus. This discourse was spoken, according to John, after Jesus had celebrated the Passover meal and instituted the holy supper. That he should speak shortly after the holy meal of himself as the Vine has special significance. The relationships of the saying to the Lord's Supper should not be lost on us. Not only have we been cleansed and purified through holy baptism and by Christ as the Word, but our Lord Jesus Christ also sustains that life for us in the Lord's Supper. As we receive in the sacrament the fruit of the vine, we receive him who is the Vine. As surely as the fruit of the vine becomes a part of us through the partaking of the supper, the Lord Jesus Christ abides in us. The Lord Jesus wanted to make that as vivid for us as he possibly could. Each time we come to the holy sacrament we receive life from the Vine.

Each time we take the Vine to ourselves by faith in the words, "given and shed for you for the remission of sins," we are cleansed and purified once more that we might produce righteousness, the fruits of holiness, to the Vinedresser. In addition to that, our Lord says, because we abide in the Savior this way, "Ask for whatever you wish, and it will be done for you." Some good-meaning folk take this to mean we get anything we want in some magical way.

It means rather, that in conformity with the suffering of our Lord, with holy baptism, with faith, and with the sacrament we can ask God for whatever we are lacking that we might be able to do what God requires of us.

The Best Fruit

Jesus concludes this portion of his discourse on a high note. Not only do those who thrive as branches on the Vine pass the judgment of the Vinedresser but they also glorify God. Jesus says, "My Father is glorified by this, that you bear much fruit and become my disciples." Does our Lord hereby contradict everything he said in the foregoing to suggest that we are saved by good works? Hardly. However, what this does suggest to us is that those works which are the product of God's love and grace do have an enduring quality.

In his book, *The Kennedy Imprisonment: A Meditation on Power,* Gary Wills contrasts the contributions of John Kennedy and Martin Luther King, Jr., through their conception of power. The Camelot that JFK created at the White House vanished. On the other hand, King, the pacifist who believed in non-violence and achievements through suffering and patience, made lasting impressions on our society. In like manner, the contrast in styles and understanding of power in ordinary people makes for differences in their lives. People who in their quiet ways draw life from the One who is the Vine discover that they not only live in him by love and grace and he in them, but also they are able to live in one another through love and grace. The restless lives of the likes of Updike's Tristao and Isabel do not have to be filled with question marks and end in dry rot. We can and do live in him who is the Vine and glorifies the Father in us.

Easter Joy

A remarkable feature of Dwight D. Eisenhower's memoirs is the composure with which he greeted crises. He titled his autobiography *At Ease,* an appropriate description for not only his retirement, but the manner in which he appeared to be on top of life. Colleagues, of course, could recall how excited he could get in revealing his impatience with mediocrity and the failures of the people in his command. However, what was impressive was the way he took control in the European theater in World War II with no fear for his own life and great confidence in the Allied offensive. One senses a greater anxiety in the young Eisenhower when he was at Camp Colt during World War I. As lieutenant colonel, Eisenhower was greatly distressed for the wholesale loss of personnel to a flu epidemic that was a threat also to him and Mamie and their infant son. In addition to the threat to their own lives, Mrs. Eisenhower lost a sister during that period.

It appeared to be one of those moments when everything was out of control. Yet Eisenhower credited a medic for special care of his family. The medic insisted that the young family be sprayed every day with some form of disinfectant. Eisenhower was not all that sure of the disinfectant but he was grateful for the attention of the medic. While Eisenhower passed over the incident, the situation does remind us of how important a role we play in each other's lives and how God works through people. That is what our Lord explains in the Holy Gospel appointed for today. Our Lord's love is to live in us that we might be able to serve one another.

God's Problem

No doubt every one of us has come to a moment in our lives when we wonder why God does not do something. There are times when it appears as though God does not care. Other times it seems like God's hands are tied. Those surmises are wrong. God always is interested and concerned about what goes on in the world. God does act in history. God does act in our personal lives. However, God must work through means and through people.

God does not act in a vacuum or in a corner. People are wrong when they ask, "Where was God?" They should ask, "Where are the people to help?" No one can say that God has not tried to get people involved. God works very hard at demonstrating God's place in history. God revealed himself in the history of the people of Israel and in the person of Jesus of Nazareth. The pressure is on us constantly to match the relevance of that history to our own lives. The history of salvation is an able demonstration of how God operates with people. God sometimes has to put people down in order to lift them up. Or, God has to allow bad times to get people's attention.

God's Solution

The clearest evidence is that God is ready with a solution to our problems. The best evidence God has given to show God's concern for the human situation is what God has done in the Person of Jesus of Nazareth. In Jesus, God became one of us. God became a child. God became a boy to live with all of the problems of being juvenile. Jesus suffered through the teen years to face all the problems of adulthood. As our Lord took his place in society, he was able to relate to the social and economic problems that develop in the communities in which people live. Jesus did not come to the world only to preach about what people should or should not do. The message our Lord shared was in essence much more. Jesus offered a message of hope and relief for people as they lived amid trials, temptations, and hardships.

Jesus lived out his own message in singular fashion. Jesus believed that God the Father was with him all the way. Jesus believed God was with him when people turned on him and made him the object of their hate, ridicule, and vengeance. Jesus refused to take matters into his own hands and to build a kingdom for himself. Jesus believed that the Heavenly Father was ruling in the world and that things would turn out right for him in spite of what people were doing to him. That is how Jesus ended up on the cross. People hated Jesus for teaching that God could be trusted in the way Jesus said. But Jesus was right. God raised Jesus from the dead to prove that God is able to bring new life out of the old, a new creation out of the old.

God Chose You

Andrew Young chose the title for his book, *The Way Out of No Way*, from an old spiritual, "I know the Lord will make a way, oh yes, he will. He'll make a way out of no way." In the concluding chapter of that remarkable book, Mr. Young confesses how his faith and the faith of his wife Jean was based on what God has done in the life of the people Israel and in the life of our Lord Jesus Christ. They experienced God's love for them when Jean was notified that she had a short time to live because of a serious problem with cancer. It was then that they went to see a doctor at Johns Hopkins whom they had learned to know when the doctor was a young lad in the civil rights movement. It was the doctor who volunteered a treatment that gave Jean a number of cancer-free years.

So it is that God uses people to accomplish acts of mercy for us, and we are called to share love in the same way. That means God chooses us for the same purpose. In holy baptism God chose us. God made us something special in God's plan for the world. Jesus took great pains to instruct the disciples in what Jesus said he had received from his Heavenly Father. In the same manner we have been so instructed. We have the materials. They are a part of our learning experience. They are of the stuff of our faith experience. It is not simply that we know a little about God. In a big way we have learned to trust God. That is the most important discovery people can make in the world.

God Loves You

What we have learned about God is that God loves us in the Lord Jesus Christ. Jesus told the disciples, "As the Father has loved me, so I have loved you." Jesus never doubted the love of the Father. That love had attended Jesus from the time of the announcement of the angel that a Holy Child was to be born of Mary. As the love of God had enveloped the life of our Lord through thick and thin all the way through the cross and tomb, Jesus was sharing that love with the disciples. They were partners with Jesus in the debates, the challenges, the dialogues, the tests, and the trials that came to Jesus daily. They lived with Jesus in the pressure tubes that were forced on Jesus. Daily the disciples witnessed how Jesus was able to cope with the hardships that came to him, because of the love of the Heavenly Father.

Jesus reminded the disciples of this when he said, "As the Father has loved me, so I have loved you." However, according to John, Jesus said this when the worst was yet to come. The disciples would not be able to endure the worst that people would do to Jesus. The terrible judgment of the crucifixion was too much for them, but not for our Lord, because of the love of the Father. After Jesus was risen from the dead the disciples could better understand this love and know that the love of the Father and of our Lord will sustain us no matter what. When we have to face the last enemy, death itself, we know that this love will carry us through that day. The love of Christ is complete. The love of Christ literally conquers all things.

Christ's Friends

Jesus was very explicit about the intensity of his love for us. Jesus said, "This is my commandment, that you love one another as I have loved you. No one has greater love than this, to lay down one's life for one's friends. You are my friends if you do what I command you. I do not call you servants any longer, because the servant does not know what the master is doing; but I have called you friends, because I have made known to you everything that I have heard from my Father."

Jesus deals with us on the most intimate terms possible. He claims to have cemented his relationship with us when he laid down his life for us. But that also put everything into a new perspective for us. By that we got in on the divine plan and scheme of things. In Christ we learned what really makes the world go around and how the Heavenly Father maintains control and works things out for the better. We are on intimate terms with God. We learn what is necessary to know. What we do not know will not hurt us. What we cannot comprehend about God or the universe is immaterial, because we know how God feels about us. What is more is that we have been made friends with God through our Lord Jesus Christ, and we are the kind of friends that God can rely on. What is more, we are the only friends that God can rely on.

Yours For The Asking

Jesus cements together all that he revealed about the love of the Father in the promise "that the Father will give you whatever you ask him in my name." We cannot ask for more than that. We are put in the enviable position of being on such intimate terms with God that we discover God to be most approachable. Judging from the popular polls that survey religious attitudes, it would appear that Americans by and large believe this to be true. The polls are so encouraging, one has to wonder if the average person does not entertain whimsical notions about how God bends us to our every desire. Certainly that is not what Jesus had in mind. What it means is that God sent Jesus into the world to reveal to us the true nature of God's love and to assure us that we are on friendly terms with God in spite of our sins and disbelief.

Jesus made it possible for us to call God "Father" in the same way as he did. In doing so, we are prompted by the Spirit of God who lives in us as God's abiding presence and love. To ask anything of the Father in the name of our Lord is to trust that God is our Father and to ask what our Lord would ask. That is far more profound than to make God some kind of errand boy who is hired to do our bidding. It is to plumb the mystery of the Holy Trinity. It is to live out what some would consider incomprehensible. Wolfhart Pannenberg, the noted German theologian, explained how the doctrine of God that appears so complicated to many can be understood in the light of the faith that recognizes how our Lord grants us his Spirit so that we might live in the trust and hope of the mercy and love of God as our Father.

You Are Appointed

With all that Jesus shared with the disciples about our privileged status with God he also stated a definite goal for us. He said, "You did not choose me but I chose you. And I appointed you to go and bear fruit, fruit that will last, so that the Father will give you whatever you ask him in my name. I am giving you these commands so that you love one another." As God sent Jesus into the world to love the world, Jesus now sends us to do the same. God must depend upon us. God needs the warm hearts and hands of people to share God's love with the world. God empowers us to bear fruit, "fruit that will last" to eternity.

William Sloane Coffin, the former chaplain at Yale University, contends that the major religious question of our day is not "What must I do to be saved?" but "What must we all do to save God's creation?" That certainly becomes more obvious day by day. For Christians who know that they are saved by God's love, the question becomes all the more imperative. What is more, Christians are gifted with the freedom and the resources of love and grace to do for God's creatures and the creation what needs to be done. The power for doing so is wrapped up in the word of our Lord, "Love one another as I have loved you."

Easter
Consecration

A. E. Hotchner has written an autobiographical account of his experience of the Great Depression. He titled this touching account of his boyhood experience in St. Louis *King of the Hill: A Memoir.* Anyone who lived through that dreadful economic period can readily recognize the painful burdens young and old had to suffer which the author describes. Anyone who did not live through that period would benefit from reading how deeply affected people were by the economic distress that appeared so relentless. Hotchner relates how as a lad he was left virtually alone to fend for himself. His brother had to be farmed out to relatives. His mother was hospitalized in a public facility for the tubercular, and his father had to hit the road to sell Elgin watches. In addition, Aaron lost other friends who had to be removed from the broken-down hotel that he called home. If that were not enough, Aaron also suffered gross disappointment in his effort to earn all of twelve dollars for a completely new graduation outfit and have money besides for the graduation party.

The young man kept a stout heart, however, by losing himself in his studies and engaging in a form of reverie. He could tell himself that all that was happening was not the way it really was. His dad and mother had another home that was quite elegant, and at the right time they would find themselves there and everything would be all right. Probably most of us have played with that form of reverie ourselves and discovered that we can lift the gloom and find determination to carry on. However, one day Aaron was invited by a neighbor to pray with her in her sorrow for the loss of her son. He confesses that he had never prayed before. Now suddenly he found new strength as he prayed for his whole family in their desperate needs. It is in God that we find not just relief through reverie, but in the very power of God's being. We learn something about that in the High Priestly prayer of our Lord in the Gospel.

An Offer

We should recognize how desperately the world needs God's help. Yet people rely on their own strength rather than looking to God for help. We can all read the ups and downs of history. The ebb and flow of history is clear and plain to us. Yet the high and the mighty appear in defiance of what God says. But their collapse is as predictable as the noses on their faces. What is not so noticeable to those who want to flaunt power and majesty is the manner in which God repeatedly lifts up the lowly. In the prayer of Jesus we learn how God lifts up the lowly.

Luther reminded us that the best way to understand this is to think of God's people as the hidden church. By that he meant to say that when you expect the power and strength of the church to be most prominent, you probably will be disappointed. On the other hand, when you are least likely to think that the church is present at all, it will rise to the occasion. God was to bring down the mighty Babylon and raise the lowly family of Hebrew exiles. We see the contemporary examples of that in the manner in which the church has emerged in China, Russia, and Eastern Germany to help effect significant changes both for the church and the world. God has a way of always keeping us guessing. Most certainly, that is obvious in the unpredictability of the elements within the creation. It is equally true of how God manages the affairs of the world. Through both fair weather and foul and also through the peace and the disturbances of the world, we must recognize that God is King. God's judgment is working on the world at all times, and the offer of God's grace is always present. It is in prayer that we reach up for the strength that God offers. Jesus teaches us how available God's grace is.

The Prayer Of Jesus

The prayer which Jesus prayed for the disciples is of excellent composition. We are not told how the evangelist was informed of the prayer. However, the prayer is of the most noble and spiritual substance. Prayed in a moment when our Lord knew that the zero hour had come for him to face his enemies and ultimately the death they would impose upon him, Jesus prayed that the Heavenly Father would strengthen him for that hour. Jesus prayed that the Father would enable him to finish and complete the work of redeeming the world in precisely the manner in which the Father had given him in order that the world might know God as the only true God and Jesus Christ whom he had sent. In the third and final portion of the prayer, Jesus prayed for the church universal and that it might come to share in the glory of our Lord.

The second portion of the prayer, which is the appointed Gospel for the day, is the petition on behalf of the disciples which is also pertinent to us as followers of the Lord Jesus. First and foremost, Jesus prayed that they might enjoy the same unity with God that the Lord Jesus knew. He prayed that they would be and could be relied upon to continue the mission of love that our Lord Jesus represented to the world. The problem with the world is that when it strives for unity it does so in human terms. Jesus made it possible for us to enjoy a unity which God himself creates. That is a unity with the Creator and the creation. That was the central purpose for our Lord's coming into the world.

Protection

Jesus prayed, "Holy Father, protect them in your name that you have given me, so that they may be one as we are one. While I was with them, I protected them in your name that you have given me." The protection our Lord was praying about was the protection against the evil one. The devil is the one who constantly harasses us and does all within that presumed power to get us into difficulty with God and with one another. The devil aims to destroy our relationship with God by making us believe that God cannot be trusted. The devil does exactly the same thing with human relations.

All reports and statistics concerning family life in our day relate over and over again how difficult human relations are in every area of life. One reason for failure in human relations is due to the fact that people are put in opposition to one another by indifference and distrust. However, what is more fundamental is that we have lost the basis for human values and priorities, because we have lost the sense of responsibility to the One who alone is able to make us at one. It is in our Creator that we discover who we are in relationship both to him and to one another. It is for this reason that Jesus prayed that we be protected from the evil one who destroys such relationships both with our Heavenly Father and with one another.

Enjoy

In contrast to how the world lives under the stress of strained human relations in families, marriages, communities, and the work place, Jesus knew the fullness of joy in his life. Jesus could say that in spite of the manner in which people opposed him and eventually persecuted and crucified him. In his prayer Jesus said to the Heavenly Father, "Now I am coming to you, and I speak these things in the world so that they may have my joy made complete in themselves." The joy of which Jesus speaks, of course, is not the kind of joy of which the world speaks. The world would have you believe that joy comes when you win the state lottery or the Ed McMahon Sweepstakes. Joy on the world's terms is supposed to come to you with the new neighborhood, the new car, or the executive's million-dollar bonus. Or the world offers joys that come with the highs on drugs, alcohol, and sensual pleasures.

Yet the same world that lures people with these illusionary offers reports daily in its own headlines the tragedies that come to people who have flirted with or tasted of these passing pleasures. When Jesus prays for us to experience his joy, he wants us to have the joy of knowing that our lives are in the hands of a gracious and tenderhearted Father who rescues us as orphans in the storm of the world. It is the discovery that our lives find their meaning in God that gives us joy. Just as Jesus could rise above all the problems that confronted him, so we also can do the same. To be able to do that is to know and experience joy.

In The World

Jesus in no way intended to make life difficult for us in the world. On the contrary, Jesus did not deny life nor the world. Jesus embraced the world fully and meant for people to have the fullness of joy in the world. Jesus prayed to the Father, "I have given them your word, and the world has hated them because they do not belong to the world, just as I do not belong to the world. I am not asking you to take them out of the world, but I ask you to protect them from the evil one." This is not double talk. Jesus means that there is much out in the world that is antagonistic toward what God has in store for God's children.

In the Gospel of John, the world is always that host of people, demons, and forces that are opposed to the gracious will of God. Thus in our families, our marriages, our communities, and the workplace there are all kinds of worldly forces that would make life difficult for us. On the other hand, Jesus says we are not to be taken out of the world, because it is in this world, this creation of God, that we are to experience and taste of the goodness of God that God has built into the creation. But we do not belong to the world in the sense that we derive our joy from the things of the world, because they are things. Rather, we see them as the gifts of God. We do not permit the evil one to spoil our enjoyment of what God does for us in the world. Jesus is not a killjoy. Jesus inspires our joy and makes the joy complete, because he not only showed us how to live in joy, but is also the source of our joy.

Sanctified

For all that Jesus prayed for us, he also prayed that God would sanctify his disciples. He prayed, "Sanctify them in the truth; your word is truth." Another word for "sanctify" is "consecrate." Either way the intention is that God should "make them holy." The children of God, who are rescued from being orphans in the world, are to be made holy even as our Lord Jesus Christ is made holy. God makes us holy as Christ is holy through what Christ has done for us. Jesus came into the world to be one of us by sharing his holiness with our humanity. By taking our flesh and identifying with us, he did us a great favor. However, that was not enough.

Jesus lived under our Law for us and died under that law that we might be declared holy in the court of God's justice. On top of all that, Jesus also rose from the dead to offer life and holiness to us. That is how we are sanctified through the word of God. Jesus is the Word himself, the word of God incarnate who shares holiness through the sacrament of Holy Baptism, the daily offer of the forgiveness of sins, and the sacrament of the Lord's supper. That means our God daily and richly sanctifies our lives in the families, in our marriages, in our communities, and in the workplace. We can carry on in spite of the onslaught of all kinds of problems, trials, temptations, and difficulties that the world poses for us, because God insulates us to the damage they can do to us through the manner in which he sanctifies us.

Sent

Jesus says to the Father that because God can and does sanctify us he sends us into the world. He prayed, "As you have sent me into the world, so I have sent them into the world. And for their sakes I sanctify myself, so that they may also be sanctified in truth." Jesus guaranteed what he was praying for by consecrating and offering himself as he did. Now then we can be sent into the world to share in the love and joy of which he prayed. Where is it better to start on this business of sharing love, grace, and forgiveness than in the home?

As we remember the special needs of dear ones and friends and the needs of all people, we pray together that all of us be consecrated as our Lord prayed. As our Lord sends us into the world, he does so in our homes first. There we experience the love of God through mothers and fathers. There we learn to socialize and carry love into the world and to share forgiveness and God's grace with the world. Our Lord himself experienced the love of

112

family and experienced the joy of the Heavenly Father. Yet our Lord did much more for the world by achieving for us what he did. He put us into the position of being able to call upon the Heavenly Father in our prayers for one another in the same manner in which he prayed this high priestly prayer for us.

You Are
My Witnesses

The inauguration of Nelson Mandela as president of the Republic of South Africa goes down in the annals of history as a most memorable moment. Imagine historians a hundred years from now trying to recreate the excitement and the significance of what took place in Pretoria and Capetown in 1994. Three centuries of bitter and harsh white rule were brought to a close as Mandela was elected the first black president by its first all-race parliament. What dramatized that election was the fact that Mr. Mandela had patiently endured 27 years of imprisonment because he protested the system of apartheid. He had refused freedom when he was offered the opportunity to return to his home province without the opportunity to actively continue his protest. His patience and hope were rewarded by those who saw fit to remove the racial barriers in order to create a truly democratic election for all the peoples of South Africa.

President Mandela is hopeful that ethnicity shall never again create oppression for any of the peoples of South Africa. Time will tell how the hoped-for ideals of the new regime will succeed in the future. However, history has very few parallels to match the experience of Mandela. To be sure, the collapse of communism in the Soviet Socialist Republics was historic, but no one emerged in quite the same way as Mr. Mandela. We can go on rummaging through history for those individuals who left dramatic impact upon their society, people, or nations, but none will match the accomplishment of the One whom we honor on this day. The ascension of our Lord Jesus Christ marked his coronation as the King of kings and Lord of lords, by which he made it possible for all peoples to know the joys of God's kingdom.

A Fulfillment

The evangelist Luke, both in his gospel and the Book of Acts, indicates how our Lord prepared his followers for the moment of his ascension. What was to take place in that instant when Jesus would be taken from the disciples was not happenstance, a sudden but happy occurrence that took place just because things fell into place. What was to transpire was a fulfillment of everything that had been written in the Hebrew Scriptures.

It was not a fulfillment just to say the ascension had been predicted. It was fulfillment in the sense that all the writings came together in him. Jesus said, "These are my words that I spoke to you while I was still with you — that everything written about me in the law of Moses, the prophets, and the psalms must be fulfilled." What God had been revealing in all those writings squared with what God did in the Person of Jesus of Nazareth. All the writings about what happened to the children of Israel and the patriarchs were about Jesus. There were not just promises about a Messiah-to-come. God was being messianic toward these people all along. Jesus personified the saving acts of God.

A Completion

Jesus explained to the disciples how it was that the scriptures were really an account about him. Luke reports, "He opened their minds to understand the scriptures, and he said to them, 'Thus it is written, that the Messiah is to suffer and to rise on the third day.'" Jesus gave the disciples a key to the reading of the scriptures in the light of his suffering and death. The life, death, and resurrection of our Lord were to be the means of being able to interpret what the scriptures are about. Their minds were opened by this process. This is what theologians have named the "analogy of faith." That is to say, that we test, measure, and relate the interpretation of the scriptures to what God has revealed in the Person and work of Jesus of Nazareth. Of late there has been a rash of materials concerning the quest of the historical Jesus.

There are books, journals, and popular articles which are upsetting for many good Christian folk because they challenge how much we can really know about the historical Jesus in the way that we keep historical records today. However, that should not be upsetting for us when we recognize how the writers of the scriptures themselves indicate to us that they are not writing biographies or historical records in the usual sense. They overtly indicate that they are recording for us that God is going to work out our salvation. Here Luke indicates that our Lord himself taught the disciples how they are to read scriptures from this point of view. What is more, Jesus was thereby indicating that this work had now been completed. Jesus had broken through the barriers to life, in breaking the spell of death on our lives, by his resurrection from the dead. The work of salvation was fulfilled and completed.

For Repentance

The purpose of the revelation which God has made in the Person of Jesus Christ was to call people to repentance. Jesus said that the Messiah was to suffer death and rise on the third day "that repentance and forgiveness of sins is to be proclaimed in his name to all nations." What God has revealed makes repentance possible. We can face up to how life really is and we can confess our part in how sinful and flawed the human condition is. We do not have to suppress how bad it is with us. We do not have to play games about how bad it can be. All that calls to mind a work by Helmut Thielicke, *Death and Life.*

Like Luther, Thielicke urged that we not set aside the contemplation of death and its reality. Luther would even say that we should be haunted by death in order to recognize it as a true judgment for sin. At the same time, Luther would help us to understand what Christ has done to overcome death for us. So Thielicke also examined the ways in which people try to repress or ignore the questions that death poses for them. He tackled the philosophers who try to make us divine, heroic, or totally pessimistic about death. However, Thielicke also attacks the way in which common people daily ignore the need of repentance in the face of death. We even have round faces on our clocks, because we know time will go around and around for us. We need to stop and think about life and death as occasions for repentance.

For Forgiveness

The death and resurrection of Jesus enable us to see that God is serious about dealing with the plight of the human condition. Jesus did not come to be a Pied Piper who could cheerily lead us through life. Nor did he come with a new prescription for better achievement for improving the world. Jesus came to deal head-on with our real problem of sin and death. He suffered the judgment of death and rose again to make it possible to believe that God is willing to set aside our sin and raise us to life eternal. That is the good news of the resurrection. The hope that we have because of the resurrection unto new life gives us new possibilities in dealing with this life. We do not have to spend time in this life fretting about the limitations of death. Nor, on the other hand, do we have to live a life of sham and hoax trying to pretend that death will not happen. God makes honest people out of us. We can deal with life as it really is and confess our sins. As repentant people we also can freely lean upon the grace and mercy of God and face up to our total dependence upon God in all that we do in this life.

Repentance and forgiveness spell freedom for us. The offer of this freedom is held out to "all nations beginning in Jerusalem," said Jesus. It was Thomas Merton who recalled for us John Donne's maxim, "No man is an island." He notes that what really binds all people together is our common search for salvation. However, he also noted that this common search is what made the French writer Sarte say, "Other people are hell." It is because people push in their own way to create their own salvation in their sinful state that they are greedy, contentious, and even warlike. People are not only divided from one another, but also divided in themselves. The only possible out we have from this condition is the offer that our Lord makes by grace that the solution comes through repentance and the forgiveness of sin.

You Are Witnesses

Jesus told the disciples that they were to be "witnesses of these things." They had been very much a part of our Lord's scene. They had been involved in his ministry. They had witnessed his death. Now they were partners with the Risen Christ in sharing the good news. Now they would be involved in a new way. He would depart from them to be with the Father. Yet he would be present with them in a new and remarkable way. They should remain in Jerusalem to receive from him the gift of the Spirit. To be sure, they had been prompted by the Spirit of God to be in his entourage to begin with.

However, now Jesus said the disciples would be "clothed with power from on high." What would happen is that all they had experienced with him and learned from him would become a part of them in a new way. They literally would be identified with all that Jesus had accomplished in such a way that they could share with others what he had shared with them. As young adults become parents they suddenly realize the powers and techniques their parents had shared with them when they were children. The new parents discover themselves to be clones of their parents saying some of the same things and attacking parental problems much the same way.

The Way is Paved

The disciples did not fail in the commission our Lord laid upon them. The fact that there is a Christian community today is testimony that they passed on what they had received. What they passed on, they did through their preaching and teaching. C. H. Dodd, a British New Testament scholar of yesteryear, surveyed their preaching in a study titled *Apostolic Preaching*. What Dodd discovered was a consistent outlining of why it was necessary for God to promise and then send God's Son among us. Then a summary of the life, death, and resurrection followed with a promise of the Holy Spirit. Beginning with the preaching of Peter in Jerusalem through the preaching and epistles of Paul, Dodd found these emphases as the heart of the apostolic message. This consistent phenomenon of itself suggested that all Christian preaching in some form should follow this pattern.

What is also obvious about the apostolic witness is that the apostles carried this message to every public forum they could. Beginning at Jerusalem where there was considerable resistance at the outset Paul, the apostle to the Gentiles, preached the same message in the public arenas of the major cities of the Mediterranean world until he finally had to address the world from prison in the imperial capital city of Rome. Now, the commission to be witnesses to this Gospel of Jesus Christ has fallen upon us. In a lecture about religion and culture, the noted author John Updike observed that one of the problems for Christianity today is that it is not seriously challenged in the public arena. If religion has gone private, it has done so to the degree that people no longer challenge it as a major threat to the culture.

Celebrate!

The Feast of the Ascension of our Lord is occasion for us to celebrate with joy and great enthusiasm. We rejoice that our Lord has taken his place with the Father to rule over the world as King of kings and Lord of lords. For us that means that our Lord has blazed the trail to eternity for us. He is the pioneer of our faith as the one who guarantees us a place with the Father. That he has entered into his glory means that he is present with us from here to eternity. All of that should mean for us that, as witnesses to his complete victory and his glory, we should engage ourselves in bold witness as to what our Lord means to us.

Crooklyn was Spike Lee's earnest attempt to relate the culture of an African-American family in Brooklyn. He portrayed the warmth, the pain, the laughter, and the heartache of a family living with the pressures of the crowded city. It is a rewarding effort to help us appreciate the strength of such a family. It is for us to apply the same kind of diligence to share with the world the gospel that enables people to transform the culture that entraps them. That is how it was for our Lord. The group of people who had been defeated and depressed by what their culture had done to them 42 days before went out with our Lord to hear his farewell. When he departed from them in the ascension into heaven, "they returned to Jerusalem with great joy, and they were continually in the temple blessing God." They knew what they had to do.

Books In This Cycle B Series

Gospel Set
God's Downward Mobility
Sermons For Advent, Christmas And Epiphany
John A. Stroman

Which Way To Jesus?
Sermons For Lent And Easter
Harry N. Huxhold

Water Won't Quench The Fire
Sermons For Pentecost (First Third)
William G. Carter

Fringe, Front And Center
Sermons For Pentecost (Middle Third)
George W. Hoyer

No Box Seats In The Kingdom
Sermons For Pentecost (Last Third)
William G. Carter

First Lesson Set
Light In The Land Of Shadows
Sermons For Advent, Christmas And Epiphany
Harold C. Warlick, Jr.

Times Of Refreshing
Sermons For Lent and Easter
E. Carver McGriff

Lyrics For The Centuries
Sermons For Pentecost (First Third)
Arthur H. Kolsti

No Particular Place To Go
Sermons For Pentecost (Middle Third)
Timothy J. Smith

When Trouble Comes!
Sermons For Pentecost (Last Third)
Zan W. Holmes, Jr.